Progress CHECK-UPS

Teacher's Manual
with Student Reproducibles

myView
LITERACY

 Pearson

Glenview, Illinois   Boston, Massachusetts
Chandler, Arizona   New York, New York

ISBN-13: 978-0-328-99049-8
ISBN-10:   0-328-99049-3

Contents

Overview and Description

OVERVIEW

The Progress Check-Ups are an important part of the wide array of formal assessments and classroom assessments that support instruction in Pearson *myView*. These check-ups are designed to measure students' progress based on the high-frequency words, phonics, comprehension, and writing taught in each week of instruction. Some items in these assessments are formatted to help students gain experience with the item format and stem language they will experience in the state test.

This Teacher's Manual includes the following: (1) a description of the Progress Check-Ups, (2) instructions for administering the check-ups, (3) instructions for scoring and recording assessment results, (4) reproducible charts on which to track students' progress, (5) item analysis charts with alignments to assessment items' skills and standards, (6) a scoring rubric for writing, (7) top-level responses for the Writing portion of each Progress Check-Up, (8) an answer key, and (9) reproducible student assessment pages.

DESCRIPTION OF THE PROGRESS CHECK-UPS

In Kindergarten, there are 25 check-ups—one for each instructional week in the Pearson *myView* program. Progress Check-Ups assess Kindergarten students in a developmentally appropriate manner. Each Progress Check-Up contains four sections.

The **High-Frequency Words** section consists of three multiple-choice questions that assess students' knowledge of the week's high-frequency words. Teacher scripting is provided for each item.

The **Phonics** section consists of four multiple-choice questions that assess students' knowledge of the week's phonics skills. Answer choices are provided as pictures, so that students do not have to be able to read. Teacher scripting is provided for each item.

The **Listening Comprehension** section consists of a selection read aloud to students and three multiple-choice questions that assess students' knowledge of the week's comprehension focus. Answer choices are provided as pictures, so that students do not have to be able to read. Teacher scripting is provided for each item.

The **Writing** section consists of a writing prompt that asks students to draw and write or dictate in a particular writing mode. You may wish to record dictation provided by students.

Administering, Scoring, and Reteaching

ADMINISTERING THE PROGRESS CHECK-UPS

The Progress Check-Ups should be administered at the end of the instruction for each week.

These assessments are not intended to be timed. However, for the purposes of scheduling, planning, and practicing for timed-assessment situations, the Progress Check-Ups can be administered in 45 minutes (approximately 15 minutes for the first two sections, 15 minutes for the Listening Comprehension section, and 15 minutes for the Writing section).

All questions and answers on all of the Kindergarten Progress Check-Ups must be read aloud to students (specific directions for administering the Progress Check-Ups can be found beginning on page T20). Before starting the assessment, make sure students understand the assessment directions and how to mark their answers. Students should answer multiple-choice items by circling the correct answer choice. Short-answer responses should be written on a separate sheet of paper. Directions in **bold** should be read aloud. Other directions are for your information.

SCORING THE PROGRESS CHECK-UPS

Reproductions of student pages containing annotated answers begin on page T70. Refer to the annotated answers for the check-up you are scoring and mark each multiple-choice question as either correct (1 point) or incorrect (0 points). To score the Writing section, refer to the rubric on page T14.

When you have finished scoring a student's Progress Check-Up, complete the appropriate row on the Student Progress Chart and the Class Progress Chart. Doing so allows you to keep track of students' total scores as well as their scores on each of the individual sections of the assessment. The chart can also help you monitor students' progress throughout the year. Refer to the Item Analysis Charts that begin on page T9 to identify what each item assesses and the Common Core State Standards aligned to each item.

RETEACHING OPTIONS

If a student receives a low score on a Progress Check-Up or shows a lack of adequate progress during the year, use *myFocus* Intervention, Level A to provide the student with additional opportunities to practice high-frequency words, phonics, comprehension, and writing. This can be done through large-group, small-group, or individual instruction. Alignments between individual assessment items and lessons in *myFocus* Intervention are provided on the Item Analysis Charts.

Student Progress Chart—Kindergarten

Name: ____

Check-Up	High-Frequency Words	Phonics	Listening Comprehension	Subtotal	Writing	TOTAL
Unit 1 Week 1	/3	/4	/3	/10		
Unit 1 Week 2	/3	/4	/3	/10		
Unit 1 Week 3	/3	/4	/3	/10		
Unit 1 Week 4	/3	/4	/3	/10		
Unit 1 Week 5	/3	/4	/3	/10		
Unit 2 Week 1	/3	/4	/3	/10		
Unit 2 Week 2	/3	/4	/3	/10		
Unit 2 Week 3	/3	/4	/3	/10		
Unit 2 Week 4	/3	/4	/3	/10		
Unit 2 Week 5	/3	/4	/3	/10		
Unit 3 Week 1	/3	/4	/3	/10		
Unit 3 Week 2	/3	/4	/3	/10		
Unit 3 Week 3	/3	/4	/3	/10		
Unit 3 Week 4	/3	/4	/3	/10		
Unit 3 Week 5	/3	/4	/3	/10		
Unit 4 Week 1	/3	/4	/3	/10		
Unit 4 Week 2	/3	/4	/3	/10		
Unit 4 Week 3	/3	/4	/3	/10		
Unit 4 Week 4	/3	/4	/3	/10		
Unit 4 Week 5	/3	/4	/3	/10		
Unit 5 Week 1	/3	/4	/3	/10		
Unit 5 Week 2	/3	/4	/3	/10		
Unit 5 Week 3	/3	/4	/3	/10		
Unit 5 Week 4	/3	/4	/3	/10		
Unit 5 Week 5	/3	/4	/3	/10		

Class Progress Chart—Kindergarten

Student's Name	Progress Check-Up Total Score																								
	U1W1	U1W2	U1W3	U1W4	U1W5	U2W1	U2W2	U2W3	U2W4	U2W5	U3W1	U3W2	U3W3	U3W4	U3W5	U4W1	U4W2	U4W3	U4W4	U4W5	U5W1	U5W2	U5W3	U5W4	U5W5

Item Analysis Charts

GRADE K, UNIT 1 PROGRESS CHECK-UP

PROGRESS CHECK-UP	SECTION	ITEMS	ITEM FOCUS/SKILL	DOK LEVEL	*myFOCUS* REMEDIATION OPPORTUNITIES	CCSS
UNIT 1 WEEK 1	Vocabulary	1–3	High-Frequency Words	Items 1–3 DOK 1	Lessons 33–35	RF.K.3.c
	Phonics	4–7	Consonant Mm (/m/) Consonant Tt (/t/)	Items 4–7 DOK 2	Lesson 21	RF.K.3.a
	Listening Comprehension	8–10	Identify and Describe Characters; Use Text Evidence	Items 8, 10 DOK 1 Item 9 DOK 2	Lesson 41	RL.K.3
	Writing	Prompt	Personal Narrative	Writing DOK 2	Lesson 53	W.K.3
UNIT 1 WEEK 2	Vocabulary	1–3	High-Frequency Words	Items 1–3 DOK 1	Lessons 33–35	RF.K.3.c
	Phonics	4–7	Short a Consonant Ss (/s/)	Items 4–7 DOK 2	Lesson 21, Lesson 25	Items 4–5 RF.K.3.b Items 6–7 RF.K.3.a
	Listening Comprehension	8–10	Describe Plot	Item 8 DOK 2 Items 9–10 DOK 1	Lesson 41	Items 8–9 RL.K.3 Item 10 RL.K.1
	Writing	Prompt	Personal Narrative	Writing DOK 3	Lesson 54	W.K.3
UNIT 1 WEEK 3	Vocabulary	1–3	High-Frequency Words	Items 1–3 DOK 1	Lessons 33–35	RF.K.3.c
	Phonics	4–7	Consonant Pp (/p/) Consonant Cc (/k/)	Items 4–7 DOK 2	Lessons 21–22	RF.K.3.a
	Listening Comprehension	8–10	Find Main Idea	Items 8–10 DOK 2	Lesson 46	RI.K.2
	Writing	Prompt	Personal Narrative	Writing DOK 3	Lesson 54	W.K.3
UNIT 1 WEEK 4	Vocabulary	1–3	High-Frequency Words	Items 1–3 DOK 1	Lessons 33–35	RF.K.3.c
	Phonics	4–7	Short i Consonant Nn (/n/)	Items 4–7 DOK 2	Lesson 22, Lesson 26	Items 4–5 RF.K.3.b Items 6–7 RF.K.3.a
	Listening Comprehension	8–10	Describe Setting	Items 8–10 DOK 2	Lesson 39, Lesson 41	RL.K.3
	Writing	Prompt	Personal Narrative	Writing DOK 3	Lesson 53	W.K.3
UNIT 1 WEEK 5	Vocabulary	1–3	High-Frequency Words	Items 1–3 DOK 1	Lessons 33–35	RF.K.3.c
	Phonics	4–7	Consonant Bb (/b/) Consonant Rr (/r/)	Items 4–7 DOK 2	Lessons 21–22	RF.K.3.a
	Listening Comprehension	8–10	Discuss Author's Purpose	Items 8–10 DOK 2	Lesson 51	RI.K.8
	Writing	Prompt	Personal Narrative	Writing DOK 3	Lesson 54	W.K.3

GRADE K, UNIT 2 PROGRESS CHECK-UP

PROGRESS CHECK-UP	SECTION	ITEMS	ITEM FOCUS/SKILL	DOK LEVEL	*myFOCUS* REMEDIATION OPPORTUNITIES	CCSS
UNIT 2 WEEK 1	Vocabulary	1–3	High-Frequency Words	Items 1–3 DOK 1	Lessons 33–35	RF.K.3.c
	Phonics	4–7	Phonics Consonant Dd (/d/) Consonant Kk (/k/)	Items 4–7 DOK 2	Lessons 22–23	RF.K.3.a
	Listening Comprehension	8–10	Find Main Idea	Items 8–10 DOK 2	Lessons 46–47	RI.K.2
	Writing	Prompt	Informational Text	Writing DOK 2	Lesson 56	W.K.3
UNIT 2 WEEK 2	Vocabulary	1–3	High-Frequency Words	Items 1–3 DOK 1	Lessons 33–35	RF.K.3.c
	Phonics	4–7	Short o Consonant Ff (/f/)	Items 4–7 DOK 1	Lesson 22, Lesson 27	RF.K.3.b
	Listening Comprehension	8–10	Find Text Structure	Items 8–10 DOK 1	Lesson 46	RI.K.2
	Writing	Prompt	Informational Text	Writing DOK 2	Lesson 56	W.K.3
UNIT 2 WEEK 3	Vocabulary	1–3	High-Frequency Words	Items 1–3 DOK 1	Lessons 33–35	RF.K.3.c
	Phonics	4–7	Consonant Hh (/h/) Consonant Ll (/l/)	Items 4–7 DOK 2	Lesson 21, Lesson 23	RF.K.3.a
	Listening Comprehension	8–10	Identify and Describe Characters	Items 8–9 DOK 1 Item 10 DOK 2	Lesson 41	RL.K.3
	Writing	Prompt	Informational Text	Writing DOK 3	Lesson 56	W.K.3
UNIT 2 WEEK 4	Vocabulary	1–3	High-Frequency Words	Items 1–3 DOK 1	Lessons 33–35	RF.K.3.c
	Phonics	4–7	Consonant Gg (/g/) Consonant Blends	Items 4–9 DOK 2	Lesson 22, Lesson 32	Items 4–5 RF.K.3.a Items 6–7 RF.K.2.d
	Listening Comprehension	8–10	Find Text Features	Items 8–9 DOK 1 Item 10 DOK 2	Lesson 46	RI.K.2
	Writing	Prompt	Informational Text	Writing DOK 3	Lesson 56	W.K.3
UNIT 2 WEEK 5	Vocabulary	1–3	High-Frequency Words	Items 1–3 DOK 1	Lessons 33–35	RF.K.3.c
	Phonics	4–7	Short e Consonants Ww (/w/) and Yy (/y/)	Items 4–7 DOK 2	Lesson 23, Lesson 28	RF.K.3.a
	Listening Comprehension	8–10	Item 8-9 Find Text Structure Item 10 Find Important Details	Items 8–10 DOK 1	Lessons 46–47	Items 8–9 RI.K.8 Item 10 RI.K.1
	Writing	Prompt	Informational Text	Writing DOK 2	Lesson 56	W.K.3

Progress Check-Ups

GRADE K, UNIT 3 PROGRESS CHECK-UP

PROGRESS CHECK-UP	SECTION	ITEMS	ITEM FOCUS/SKILL	DOK LEVEL	*myFOCUS* REMEDIATION OPPORTUNITIES	CCSS
UNIT 3 WEEK 1	Vocabulary	1–3	High-Frequency Words	Items 1–3 DOK 1	Lessons 33–35	RF.K.3.c
	Phonics	4–7	Consonant Jj (/j/) Consonant Xx (/ks/)	Items 4–7 DOK 2	Lesson 23	RF.K.3.a
	Listening Comprehension	8–10	Discuss Theme	Items 8–10 DOK 2	Lesson 38	RL.K.1
	Writing	Prompt	Fiction	Writing DOK 3	Lesson 56	W.K.5
UNIT 3 WEEK 2	Vocabulary	1–3	High-Frequency Words	Items 1–3 DOK 1	Lessons 33–35	RF.K.3.c
	Phonics	4–7	Short u Consonant Vv (/v/)	Items 4–7 DOK 2	Lesson 23, Lesson 29	Item 4 RF.K.3.b Items 5–7 RF.K.3.a
	Listening Comprehension	8–10	Items 8–9 Compare and Contrast Stories Item 10 Make Inferences	Items 8–10 DOK 2	Lesson 41	Items 8–9 RL.K.9 Item 10 RL.K.3
	Writing	Prompt	Fiction	Writing DOK 3	Lesson 56	W.K.5
UNIT 3 WEEK 3	Vocabulary	1–3	High-Frequency Words	Items 1–3 DOK 1	Lessons 33–35	RF.K.3.c
	Phonics	4–7	Consonant Zz (/z/) Consonant Qq (/kw/)	Items 4–7 DOK 2	Lesson 23	RF.K.3.a
	Listening Comprehension	8–10	Discuss Rhyme and Rhythm Ask and Answer Questions	Items 8–10 DOK 2	Lesson 40, Lesson 44	RL.K.5
	Writing	Prompt	Fiction	Writing DOK 3	Lesson 56	W.K.1
UNIT 3 WEEK 4	Vocabulary	1–3	High-Frequency Words	Items 1–3 DOK 1	Lessons 33–35	RF.K.3.c
	Phonics	4–7	Short a Long Aa (/ā/)	Items 4–7 DOK 2	Lesson 25, Lesson 30	RF.K.3.b
	Listening Comprehension	8–10	Items 8–9 Discuss Author's Purpose Item 10 Main Idea	Items 8–9 DOK 2 Item 10 DOK 2	Lesson 39	RL.K.6
	Writing	Prompt	Fiction	Writing DOK 3	Lesson 56	W.K.1
UNIT 3 WEEK 5	Vocabulary	1–3	High-Frequency Words	Items 1–3 DOK 1	Lessons 33–35	RF.K.3.c
	Phonics	4–7	Long i Short i	Items 4–7 DOK 2	Lesson 26, Lesson 30	RF.K.3.b
	Listening Comprehension	8–10	Describe Plot	Items 8–10 DOK 1	Lesson 41	RL.K.3
	Writing	Prompt	Fiction	Writing DOK 3	Lesson 56	W.K.1

GRADE K, UNIT 4 PROGRESS CHECK-UP

PROGRESS CHECK-UP	SECTION	ITEMS	ITEM FOCUS/SKILL	DOK LEVEL	myFOCUS REMEDIATION OPPORTUNITIES	CCSS
UNIT 4 WEEK 1	Vocabulary	1–3	High-Frequency Words	Items 1–3 DOK 1	Lessons 33–35	RF.K.3.c
	Phonics	4–7	Short Oo (/o/); Long Oo (/ō/)	Items 4–7 DOK 2	Lesson 25, Lesson 30	RF.K.3.b
	Listening Comprehension	8–10	Describe Connections Find Important Details	Items 8–10 DOK 2	Lessons 47–48	RI.K.3
	Writing	Prompt	Personal Narrative	Writing DOK 3	Lesson 56	W.K.3
UNIT 4 WEEK 2	Vocabulary	1–3	High-Frequency Words	Items 1–3 DOK 1	Lessons 33–35	RF.K.3.c
	Phonics	4–7	Short Uu (/u/) Long Uu (/ū/)	Items 4–7 DOK 2	Lesson 29, Lesson 31	RF.K.3.b
	Listening Comprehension	8–10	Find Main Idea Make Inferences	Items 8–10 DOK 2	Lesson 46, Lesson 48	Items 8–9 RI.K.2 Item 10 RI.K.1
	Writing	Prompt	Personal Narrative	Writing DOK 3	Lesson 56	W.K.1
UNIT 4 WEEK 3	Vocabulary	1–3	High-Frequency Words	Items 1–3 DOK 1	Lessons 33–35	RF.K.3.c
	Phonics	4–7	Short Ee (/e/) Long Ee (/ē/)	Items 4–7 DOK 2	Lesson 28, Lesson 31	RF.K.3.b
	Listening Comprehension	8–10	Describe Setting	Items 8–10 DOK 1	Lesson 41	RL.K.3
	Writing	Prompt	Personal Narrative	Writing DOK 3	Lesson 56	W.K.3
UNIT 4 WEEK 4	Vocabulary	1–3	High-Frequency Words	Items 1–3 DOK 1	Lessons 33–35	RF.K.3.c
	Phonics	4–7	Review and Reinforce (Pp, Yy, Short and Long i)	Items 4–7 DOK 2	Lesson 21, Lesson 23, Lesson 26	RF.K.3.b
	Listening Comprehension	8–10	Find Text Features	Items 8–10 DOK 2	Lesson 46	RI.K.3
	Writing	Prompt	Personal Narrative	Writing DOK 3	Lesson 56	W.K.3
UNIT 4 WEEK 5	Vocabulary	1–3	High-Frequency Words	Items 1–3 DOK 1	Lessons 33–35	RF.K.3.c
	Phonics	4–7	Review and Reinforce (Dd, Ff, Vv, Short e)	Items 4–7 DOK 2	Lesson 22, Lesson 23, Lesson 28	RF.K.3.b
	Listening Comprehension	8–10	Determine Theme Ask and Answer Questions	Items 8–10 DOK 2	Lesson 39, Lesson 44	RL.K.3
	Writing	Prompt	Personal Narrative	Writing DOK 3	Lesson 56	W.K.3

GRADE K, UNIT 5 PROGRESS CHECK-UP

PROGRESS CHECK-UP	SECTION	ITEMS	ITEM FOCUS/SKILL	DOK LEVEL	myFOCUS REMEDIATION OPPORTUNITIES	CCSS
UNIT 5 WEEK 1	Vocabulary	1–3	High-Frequency Words	Items 1–3 DOK 1	Lessons 33–35	RF.K.3.c
	Phonics	4–7	Cc, Tt, Short o, Long o	Items 4–6 DOK 2; Item 7 DOK 2	Lessons 21–23, Lesson 28	Items 4–5 RF.K.3.a Items 6–7 RF.K.3.b
	Listening Comprehension	8–10	Connect Texts and Illustrations Use Text Evidence	Items 8–10 DOK 2	Lesson 47, Lesson 49	Items 8–9 RI.K.7 Item 10 RL.K1
	Writing	Prompt	Literary Nonfiction	Writing DOK 2	Lesson 56	W.K.2
UNIT 5 WEEK 2	Vocabulary	1–3	High-Frequency Words	Items 1–3 DOK 1	Lessons 33–35	RF.K.3.c
	Phonics	4–7	Bb, Jj, Initial and Final Blends	Items 4–7 DOK 2	Lessons 22–23, Lesson 32	Items 4–5 RF.K.3.a Items 5–7 RF.K.2.d
	Listening Comprehension	8–10	Find Text Structure Find Important Details	Items 8–10 DOK 1	Lessons 46–47	Items 8–9 RI.K.3 Item 10 RI.K.3
	Writing	Prompt	Literary Nonfiction	Writing DOK 3	Lesson 56	W.K.5
UNIT 5 WEEK 3	Vocabulary	1–3	High-Frequency Words	Items 1–3 DOK 1	Lessons 33–35	RF.K.3.c
	Phonics	4–7	Gg, Qq, Short a, Long a	Items 4–7 DOK 2	Lessons 22–23, Lesson 25, Lesson 30	Items 4–5 RF.K.3.a Items 6–7 RF.K.3.b
	Listening Comprehension	8–10	Discuss Rhyme and Rhythm	Items 8–10 DOK 2	Lesson 40	RL.K.5
	Writing	Prompt	Literary Nonfiction	Writing DOK 2	Lesson 56	W.K.2
UNIT 5 WEEK 4	Vocabulary	1–3	High-Frequency Words	Items 1–3 DOK 1	Lessons 33–35	RF.K.3.c
	Phonics	4–7	Consonants Kk, Ss, Ww, Mm	Items 4–7 DOK 2	Lessons 21–23	RF.K.3.a
	Listening Comprehension	8–10	Compare and Contrast Texts	Items 8–10 DOK 2	Lesson 52	RI.K.9
	Writing	Prompt	Literary Nonfiction	Writing DOK 2	Lesson 56	W.K.2
UNIT 5 WEEK 5	Vocabulary	1–3	High-Frequency Words	Items 1–3 DOK 1	Lessons 33–35	RF.K.3.c
	Phonics	4–7	Consonants Ll, Rr, Nn, Zz	Items 4–7 DOK 2	Lessons 21–22, Lesson 24	RF.K.3.a
	Listening Comprehension	8–10	Discuss Characters in Drama	Items 8–10 DOK 2	Lesson 40	RL.K.3
	Writing	Prompt	Literary Nonfiction	Writing DOK 3	Lesson 56	W.K.2

Writing Rubric

Use the following rubric to evaluate responses on the Writing section of each Progress Check-Up. Suggested top-score responses for each prompt follow the rubric.

SCORE	FOCUS	ORGANIZATION	DEVELOPMENT	LANGUAGE AND VOCABULARY	CONVENTIONS
4	Drawing/text/oral response is focused on an appropriate idea or topic.	Drawing/text/oral response is clear, organized, and logical.	Drawing/text/oral response uses details, descriptions, and/or facts.	Text/oral response uses appropriate, relevant, and precise language.	Text flows from left to right and has correct grammar, usage, spelling, capitalization, and punctuation.
3	Drawing/text/oral response is mostly focused on an appropriate idea or topic.	Drawing/text/oral response is mostly clear, organized, and logical.	Drawing/text/oral response uses some details, descriptions, and/or facts.	Text/oral response uses mostly appropriate, relevant, and precise language.	Text mostly flows from left to right and has a few conventions errors but is understandable.
2	Drawing/text/oral response is somewhat focused on an appropriate idea or topic.	Drawing/text/oral response shows some organization.	Drawing/text/oral response uses few details, descriptions, and/or facts.	Text/oral response may use inappropriate, imprecise, irrelevant, or overly simple language.	Text sometimes flows from left to right and has some conventions errors.
1	Drawing/text/oral response is unfocused, confusing, or inappropriate.	Drawing/text/oral response has no organization.	Drawing/text/oral response uses very few or no details, descriptions, and/or facts.	Text/oral response uses vague, confusing, inappropriate, or irrelevant language.	Text does not flow from left to right or is hard to follow because of many conventions errors.
0	The drawing/text/oral response gets no credit if it does not demonstrate adequate command of the traits of the mode of writing.				

Top-Level Responses for Writing

UNIT 1

Unit 1, Week 1 Writing

The personal narrative should:

- include a picture about something the writer would like to do
- include an oral or written sentence describing the picture
- follow the structure of a personal narrative

Unit 1, Week 2 Writing

The personal narrative should:

- include a picture of two ways to learn one's way around a new place
- include an oral or written sentence describing the picture
- follow the structure of a personal narrative

Unit 1, Week 3 Writing

The personal narrative should:

- include a picture about a place the writer likes to go to and something they see there
- include an oral or written sentence describing the picture
- follow the structure of a personal narrative

Unit 1, Week 4 Writing

The personal narrative should:

- include a picture of what the writer might see at a planetarium
- include an oral or written sentence describing the picture
- follow the structure of personal narrative .

Unit 1, Week 5 Writing

The personal narrative should:

- include a picture of something the writer might see at a farmers market
- include an oral or written sentence describing the picture
- follow the structure of a personal narrative

UNIT 2

Unit 2, Week 1 Writing

The informational text should:

- include a picture of an animal
- include an oral or written sentence with a detail about the animal
- follow the structure of an informational text

Unit 2, Week 2 Writing

The informational text should:

- include a picture of an animal home
- include the name of the animal that lives in the home in writing or orally
- follow the structure of an informational text

Unit 2, Week 3 Writing

The informational text should:

- include a picture of something the writer likes to wear
- include an oral or written sentence telling one detail about what the writer likes to wear
- follow the structure of an informational text

Unit 2, Week 4 Writing

The informational text should:

- include a picture of an animal
- include an oral or written sentence describing one food the writer thinks the animal eats
- follow the structure of an informational text

Unit 2, Week 5 Writing

The informational text should:

- include a picture of the writer's favorite way to play
- include an oral or written sentence describing three ways the writer likes to play
- follow the structure of an informational text

UNIT 3

Unit 3, Week 1 Writing

The fiction writing should:

- include a picture of the characters and setting of a fiction story the writer would like to write
- include an oral or written sentence about an event from the story
- follow the structure of fiction writing

Unit 3, Week 2 Writing

The fiction writing should:

- include a picture of a story from the writer's life
- include an oral or written list of three things that happened in the story
- follow the structure of fiction writing

Unit 3, Week 3 Writing

The fiction writing should:

- include a picture of the writer's favorite fiction book
- include an oral or written sentence describing the events from the beginning and end of the book
- follow the structure of fiction writing

Unit 3, Week 4 Writing

The fiction writing should:

- include a picture of a make-believe person the writer would like to tell a story about
- include an oral or written sentence describing one thing the person would do in the story
- follow the structure of fiction writing

Unit 3, Week 5 Writing

The fiction writing should:

- include a picture of Pegasus
- include an oral or written sentence describing something Pegasus could do in a story
- follow the structure of fiction writing

UNIT 4

Unit 4, Week 1 Writing

The personal narrative should:

- include a picture of what the writer most likes to draw in his or her favorite color
- include an oral or written sentence describing the drawing and the writer's favorite color
- follow the structure of a personal narrative

Unit 4, Week 2 Writing

The personal narrative should:

- include a picture of the writer's favorite place
- include an oral or written sentence describing the place
- follow the structure of a personal narrative

Unit 4, Week 3 Writing

The personal narrative should:

- include a picture of a problem the writer had to solve
- include an oral or written sentence describing the steps the writer took to solve the problem
- follow the structure of a personal narrative

Unit 4, Week 4 Writing

The personal narrative should:

- include a picture about something the writer would like to do when he or she grows up
- include an oral or written sentence that describes what the writer would like to do when he or she grows up
- follow the structure of a personal narrative

Unit 4, Week 5 Writing

The personal narrative should:

- include a picture of a tradition the writer has with his or her family
- include two oral or written sentences describing the tradition
- follow the structure of a personal narrative

UNIT 5

Unit 5, Week 1 Writing

The literary nonfiction text should:

- include a picture of a weather event
- include an oral or written sentence describing the weather event
- follow the structure of literary nonfiction

Unit 5, Week 2 Writing

The literary nonfiction text should:

- include a picture of a tree during one of the seasons
- include an oral or written sentence describing the tree
- follow the structure of literary nonfiction

Unit 5, Week 3 Writing

The literary nonfiction text should:

- include a picture of something the writer likes to do when it rains
- include an oral or written sentence describing what the writer likes to do when it rains
- follow the structure of literary nonfiction

Unit 5, Week 4 Writing

The literary nonfiction text should:

- include a picture of something the writer wears in the summer
- include a complete sentence about what he or she does when wearing those clothes
- follow the structure of literary nonfiction

Unit 5, Week 5 Writing

The literary nonfiction text should:

- include a picture of something the writer might do if it snowed
- include a complete sentence describing the activity
- follow the structure of literary nonfiction

Teacher Scripting: Unit 1 Week 1 Progress Check-Up

HIGH-FREQUENCY WORDS

Turn to page 1. Use the following directions to administer the assessment. Directions in bold are to be read aloud. The others are for your information only. Students are to respond by circling the answer to each question.

Move through the assessment quickly to make sure you are assessing the student's ability to recognize the high-frequency words.

Look at the first page. I am going to say a word in each row, and you are going to circle the word I am saying.

1. **Find the square at the top of the page. Put your finger on the square. Now look at the three words in that row. Draw a circle around the word *I...I.***

2. **Move down to the next row. Find the circle. Put your finger on it. Now look at the three words in that row. Draw a circle around the word *the...the.***

3. **Move down to the next row. Find the triangle. Put your finger on it. Now look at the three words in that row. Draw a circle around the word *am...am.***

PHONICS

Turn to page 2. Move through this assessment a bit more slowly than you did for high-frequency words. The students will need more time to answer these questions.

Turn to the second page. I will tell you the sound a letter makes, and you will circle the picture of the word with that sound.

1. **Find the square at the top of the page. Put your finger on it. Now look at the three pictures in that row: *jar...monkey...sock*. The letter *m* makes the sound /m/. Draw a circle around the picture that has the beginning /m/ sound: *jar...monkey...sock*.**

2. **Move down to the next row of pictures where you see the circle. Put your finger on it. Now look at the three pictures in that row: *milk...fish...rake*. The letter *m* makes the sound /m/. Draw a circle around the picture that has the beginning /m/ sound: *milk...fish...rake*.**

3. **Move down to the next row of pictures where you see the triangle. Put your finger on it. Now look at the three pictures in that row: *bag...turtle...cake*. The letter *t* makes the sound /t/. Draw a circle around the picture that has the beginning /t/sound: *bag...turtle...cake*.**

4. **Move down to the next row of pictures where you see the heart. Put your finger on it. Now look at the three pictures in that row: *table...wagon...snake*. The letter *t* makes the sound /t/. Draw a circle around the picture that has the beginning /t/ sound: *table...wagon...snake*.**

LISTENING COMPREHENSION

Turn to page 3. You will read a selection and comprehension questions to the students.

Turn to the last page of your assessment. Now I will read a selection about daydreaming. Then I will ask you some questions. Listen carefully. Here is the selection.

Underwater World

Thomas lies down on his bed. He imagines standing on the edge of a big boat. He is wearing a mask that will let him see underwater. He will breathe air from tanks on his back. Splash! Into the water Thomas goes.

In his mind, Thomas kicks his feet and begins to swim underwater. He looks through the mask. What will he see first?

Fish! There are red fish, blue fish, and yellow fish. There is a fish that is all puffed out like a balloon! And look! A tiny seahorse is gliding through the water. Thomas wishes it was bigger.

Now, what's over here? It looks like long, tall grass. Thomas knows it is seaweed. *It's waving to me,* thinks Thomas. He waves back.

"Thomas? Thomas?" Thomas hears his mother's voice. "Why, you have hardly started cleaning your room! Are you daydreaming again?"

Thomas sighs. The rest of his ocean adventure will have to wait.

Now I will ask you some questions about the selection. For each question, there are three pictures in a row. Draw a circle around the picture that shows the best answer. Listen carefully.

1. **Find the square at the top of the page and put your finger on it. Now look at the three pictures in that row. Who is the main character in the selection? — *a boy...a fish...a mother?* Circle the picture that shows who the selection is about mostly about.**

2. **Move down to the next row. Find the circle. Put your finger on it. What is the main character daydreaming about? — *playing...swimming...walking?* Circle the picture that shows what the main character is daydreaming about.**

3. **Move down to the next row. Find the triangle. Put your finger on it. Where would the main character like to go? — *in a boat...underwater...a room?* Circle the picture that shows where the main character would like to go.**

WRITING

On a separate sheet of paper, students will draw a picture about something they would like to do and then dictate a sentence that tells about the story. Record the sentence under the picture.

Teacher Scripting: Unit 1 Week 2 Progress Check-Up

HIGH-FREQUENCY WORDS

Turn to page 4. Use the following directions to administer the assessment. Directions in bold are to be read aloud. The others are for your information only. Students are to respond by circling the answer to each question.

Move through the assessment quickly to make sure you are assessing the child's ability to recognize the high-frequency words.

Look at the first page. I am going to say a word in each row, and you are going to circle the word I am saying.

1. **Find the square at the top of the page. Put your finger on the square. Now look at the three words in that row. Draw a circle around the word *like...like*.**

2. **Move down to the next row. Find the circle. Put your finger on it. Now look at the three words in that row. Draw a circle around the word *to...to*.**

3. **Move down to the next row. Find the triangle. Put your finger on it. Now look at the three words in that row. Draw a circle around the word *a...a*.** [To the Teacher: Use the long *a* sound.]

PHONICS

Turn to page 5. Move through this assessment more slowly than you did for high-frequency words. The students will need more time to answer these questions.

Turn to the second page. I will tell you the sound a letter makes, and you will circle the picture of the word with that sound.

1. **Find the square at the top of the page. Put your finger on it. Now look at the three pictures in that row: *cat...bus...shovel*. The letter *a* makes the sound /a/. Draw a circle around the picture that has the /a/ sound: *cat...bus...shovel*.**

2. **Move down to the next row of pictures where you see the circle. Put your finger on it. Now look at the three pictures in that row: *pan...book...mop*. The letter *a* makes the sound /a/. Draw a circle around the picture that has the /a/ sound: *pan...book...mop*.**

3. **Move down to the next row of pictures where you see the triangle. Put your finger on it. Now look at the three pictures in that row: *dish...boot...sunflower*. The letter *s* makes the sound /s/. Draw a circle around the picture that has the beginning /s/ sound: *dish...boot...sunflower*.**

4. **Move down to the next row of pictures where you see the heart. Put your finger on it. Now look at the three pictures in that row: *dog...sailboat...corn*. The letter *s* makes the sound /s/. Draw a circle around the picture that has the beginning /s/ sound: *dog...sailboat...corn*.**

LISTENING COMPREHENSION

Turn to page 6. You will read a selection and comprehension questions to the students.

Turn to the last page of your assessment. Now I will read a selection about discovering new places and people. Then I will ask some questions. Listen carefully. Here is the selection.

Lost and Found

"Rosa, hurry up! We are going to be late to William's party!" said her brother Steven. Steven was excited. They had just moved into town a few weeks earlier. A new friend at school had invited Steven, Rosa, and their mother to his birthday party.

The three set off after their mother locked the door with her key.

"Now, where do we go when we get to the corner?" said their mother.

"Wait a minute," said Steven. "I have the directions in my pocket." Steven looked into his jacket pocket. Then he looked in his pants pocket.

"Oh, no, Steven!" said Rosa. "You forgot the directions! What are we going to do now?" Steven looked very sad. He sat on the grass and watched a policeman direct traffic. *Can anyone help us?* he wondered. Just then, they saw a red balloon floating in the air. Joe, a friend of Steven's from school, was holding it.

"Hello" said Joe. "Are you on your way to William's party?"

"Yes, Joe. But Steven lost the directions." said Rosa.

"Follow me," said Joe. "It's just one block away. It will be great fun!"

Now I will ask you some questions about the selection. For each question, there are three pictures in a row. Draw a circle around the picture that shows the best answer. Listen carefully.

1. **Find the square at the top of the page and put your finger on it. Now look at the three pictures in that row. What is the selection about? — *taking a walk...playing with a dog...going to a party?* Circle the picture that shows what the selection is mostly about.**

2. **Move down to the next row. Find the circle. Put your finger on it. What happens to Steven on the way to William's birthday party? — *he loses the directions...he forgets William's gift...he loses the house key?* Circle the picture that shows what happened to Steven on the way to William's birthday party.**

3. **Move down to the next row. Find the triangle. Put your finger on it. Who helps Steven, Rosa, and their mother with their problem? — *a policeman...a neighbor...a school friend?* Circle the picture that shows who helps Steven, Rosa, and their mother.**

WRITING

On a sheet of paper, students will draw two ways to learn their way around a new place. Then they will write or tell something about their drawings. Record the sentences under the picture.

HIGH-FREQUENCY WORDS

Turn to page 7. Use the following directions to administer the assessment. Directions in bold are to be read aloud. The others are for your information only. Students are to respond by circling the answer to each question.

Move through the assessment quickly to make sure you are assessing the student's ability to recognize the high-frequency words.

Look at the first page. I am going to say a word in each row, and you are going to circle the word I am saying.

1. **Find the square at the top of the page. Put your finger on the square. Now look at the three words in that row. Draw a circle around the word** *have…have.*

2. **Move down to the next row. Find the circle. Put your finger on it. Now look at the three words in that row. Draw a circle around the word** *he…he.*

3. **Move down to the next row. Find the triangle. Put your finger on it. Now look at the three words in that row. Draw a circle around the word** *is…is.*

PHONICS

Turn to page 8. Move through this assessment more slowly than you did for high-frequency words. The students will need more time to answer these questions.

Turn to the second page. I will tell you the sound a letter makes, and you will circle the picture of the word with that sound.

1. **Find the square at the top of the page. Put your finger on it. Now look at the three pictures in that row:** *pumpkin…bat…shoe.* **The letter** *p* **makes the sound /p/. Draw a circle around the picture that has the beginning /p/ sound:** *pumpkin…bat…shoe.*

2. **Move down to the next row of pictures where you see the circle. Put your finger on it. Now look at the three pictures in that row:** *duck…ball…pail.* **The letter** *p* **makes the sound /p/. Draw a circle around the picture that has the beginning /p/ sound:** *duck…ball…pail.*

3. **Move down to the next row of pictures where you see the triangle. Put your finger on it. Now look at the three pictures in that row:** *carrot…box…sun.* **The letter** *c* **makes the sound /k/. Draw a circle around the picture that has the beginning /k/ sound:** *carrot…box…sun.*

4. **Move down to the next row of pictures where you see the heart. Put your finger on it. Now look at the three pictures in that row:** *apple…corn…door.* **The letter** *c* **makes the sound /k/. Draw a circle around the picture that has the beginning /k/ sound:** *apple…corn…door.*

LISTENING COMPREHENSION

Turn to page 9. You will read a selection and comprehension questions to the students.

Turn to the last page of your assessment. Now I will read a selection about lighthouses. Then I will ask you some questions. Listen carefully. Here is the selection.

Lighthouses!

People have used ships to go to faraway places for a long time. In the past, this way of traveling was much different than it is now. During the day, a person steering a ship could keep it away from the rocks near land. But at night, it was too dark to see those rocks. A ship might smash into them.

A big fire near the shore could help people on a ship see where the land was, so they could steer away from it. Even better was a tall tower, called a lighthouse, with a bright light shining out of windows at the top. This light, called a beacon, is like a big flashlight that warns people of danger. Before electric lights were invented, candles were used to produce the light in a beacon.

Lighthouses were built near rocky parts of coasts and on islands. Today, there are still many lighthouses shining their lights out over the water to keep the people at sea safe, just as they have for hundreds of years.

Now I will ask you some questions about the selection. For each question, there are three pictures in a row. Draw a circle around the picture that shows the best answer. Listen carefully.

1. **Find the square at the top of the page and put your finger on it. Now look at the three pictures in that row. What is the selection mostly about? — *boats...lighthouses... islands?* Circle the picture that shows what the selection is mostly about.**

2. **Move down to the next row. Find the circle. Put your finger on it. Before there were lighthouses, what did people use to help people on ships see nearby dangers? — *a fire...a flashlight...a window?* Circle the picture that shows what people used before lighthouses to help keep ships safe.**

3. **Move down to the next row. Find the triangle. Put your finger on it. What does the selection say has been used for hundreds of years to keep people at sea safe? — *computers...candles ...lighthouses?* Circle the picture that shows what the selection says has been used for hundreds of years to keep people at sea safe.**

WRITING

On a separate sheet of paper, students will draw a picture of a real place they like to go to or something they see there and then dictate a sentence that tells something about what they have drawn. Record the sentence under the picture.

HIGH-FREQUENCY WORDS

Turn to page 10. Use the following directions to administer the assessment. Directions in bold are to be read aloud. The others are for your information only. Students are to respond by circling the answer to each question.

Move through the assessment quickly to make sure you are assessing the student's ability to recognize the high-frequency words.

Look at the first page. I am going to say a word in each row, and you are going to circle the word I am saying.

1. **Find the square at the top of the page. Put your finger on the square. Now look at the three words in that row. Draw a circle around the word *we...we*.**

2. **Move down to the next row. Find the circle. Put your finger on it. Now look at the three words in that row. Draw a circle around the word *my...my*.**

3. **Move down to the next row. Find the triangle. Put your finger on it. Now look at the three words in that row. Draw a circle around the word *make...make*.**

PHONICS

Turn to page 11. Move through this assessment more slowly than you did for high-frequency words. The students will need more time to answer these questions.

Turn to the second page. I will tell you the sound a letter makes, and you will circle the picture of the word with that sound.

1. **Find the square at the top of the page. Put your finger on it. Now look at the three pictures in that row: *kid...pear...kite*. The letter *i* makes the short *i* sound /i/. Draw a circle around the picture that has the short *i* sound /i/: *kid...pear...kite*.**

2. **Move down to the next row of pictures where you see the circle. Now look at the three pictures in that row: *boat...fish...sky*. The letter *i* makes the short *i* sound /i/. Draw a circle around the picture that has the short *i* sound /i/: *boat...fish...sky*.**

3. **Move down to the next row of pictures where you see the triangle. Put your finger on it. Now look at the three pictures in that row: *nine...clock...bird*. The letter *n* makes the sound /n/. Draw a circle around the picture that has the beginning /n/ sound: *nine...clock...bird*.**

4. **Move down to the next row of pictures where you see the heart. Put your finger on it. Now look at the three pictures in that row: *drum...net...carrot*. The letter *n* makes the sound /n/. Draw a circle around the picture that has the beginning /n/ sound: *drum...net...carrot*.**

LISTENING COMPREHENSION

Turn to page 12. You will read a selection and comprehension questions to the students.

Turn to the last page of your assessment. Now I am going to read a selection about a special class trip. Then I will ask you some questions. Listen carefully. Here is the selection.

Seeing Stars

Leah was very excited. Today, her class was going to visit the city planetarium.

**"Who remembers what a planetarium is?" her teacher asked the class.
Leah raised her hand. Her teacher called on her. "A planetarium is a building like a movie theater. You go there to learn about planets and stars."**

"That's right. Today, we will watch a special movie about the night sky."

Leah and her classmates left their classroom and got on a bus. The bus took them to the planetarium. A woman named Dr. Thomas explained that with the help of a special movie projector, she would teach them about the sky. Leah liked to look at stars. On clear nights, she and her grandfather looked at through a telescope.

The class took their seats. The lights turned low. They looked up and it was just like looking up at the night sky! Dr. Thomas taught them many interesting things about the planets and stars.

Now I will ask you some questions about the selection. For each question, there are three pictures in a row. Draw a circle around the picture that shows the best answer. Listen carefully.

1. **Find the square at the top of the page and put your finger on it. Now look at the three pictures in that row. Where did the class visit? —** *a school...a house...a planetarium?* **Circle the picture that shows where the class visited.**

2. **Move down to the next row. Find the circle. Put your finger on it. Before going to the planetarium, how did Leah see stars with her grandfather? —** *with a telescope ...with a camera...with a projector?* **Circle the picture that shows how Leah first saw stars.**

3. **Move down to the next row. Find the triangle. Put your finger on it. Where is Leah at the beginning of the story? —** *outside...at a movie theater...in a classroom?*

WRITING

On a separate sheet of paper, students will draw a picture of something they might see at a planetarium. Then they will write or dictate something about the drawing. Record the sentences under the picture.

Teacher Scripting: Unit 1 Week 5 Progress Check-Up

HIGH-FREQUENCY WORDS

Turn to page 13. Use the following directions to administer the assessment. Directions in bold are to be read aloud. The others are for your information only. Students are to respond by circling the answer to each question.

Move through the assessment quickly to make sure you are assessing the student's ability to recognize the high-frequency words.

Look at the first page. I am going to say a word in each row, and you are going to circle the word I am saying.

1. **Find the square at the top of the page. Put your finger on the square. Now look at the three words in that row. Draw a circle around the word *for...for*.**

2. **Move down to the next row. Find the circle. Put your finger on it. Now look at the three words in that row. Draw a circle around the word *me...me*.**

3. **Move down to the next row. Find the triangle. Put your finger on it. Now look at the three words in that row. Draw a circle around the word *with...with*.**

PHONICS

Turn to page 14. Move through this assessment a bit more slowly than you did for high-frequency words. The students will need more time to answer these questions.

Turn to the second page. I will tell you about the sound a letter makes, and you will circle the picture of the word with that sound.

1. **Find the square at the top of the page. Put your finger on it. Now look at the three pictures in that row: *bicycle...cow...dress*. The letter *b* makes the sound /b/. Draw a circle around the picture that has the beginning /b/ sound: *bicycle...cow...dress*.**

2. **Move down to the next row of pictures where you see the circle. Put your finger on it. Now look at the three pictures in that row: *star...bell...frog*. The letter *b* makes the sound /b/. Draw a circle around the picture that has the beginning /b/ sound: *star... bell...frog*.**

3. **Move down to the next row of pictures where you see the triangle. Put your finger on it. Now look at the three pictures in that row: *log...rope...bag*. The letter *r* makes the sound /r/. Draw a circle around the picture that has the beginning /r/ sound: *log...rope...bag*.**

4. **Move down to the next row of pictures where you see the heart. Put your finger on it. Now look at the three pictures in that row: *rabbit...milk...apple*. The letter *r* makes the sound /r/. Draw a circle around the picture that has the beginning /r/ sound: *rabbit...milk...apple***

LISTENING COMPREHENSION

Turn to page 15. You will read a selection and comprehension questions to the students.

Turn to the last page of your assessment. Now I will read a selection about farmers markets. Then I will ask you some questions. Listen carefully. Here is the selection.

Let's Go to the Farmers Market

People go to farmers markets to buy fresh fruit and vegetables to eat. Farmers who live nearby grow almost all of the food found at a farmers market.

Farmers grow different foods at different times of the year. For example, there might be strawberries in May! In October, there might be pumpkins and spinach.

You can buy more than fruits and vegetables at a farmers market. Some farmers sell fresh eggs. You might be able to buy pies and breads.

Farmers markets are important. People can buy fresh food and learn about farms. Farmers can sell the things they grow.

Now I will ask you some questions about the selection. For each question, there are three pictures in a row. Draw a circle around the picture that shows the best answer. Listen carefully.

1. **Find the square at the top of the page and put your finger on it. Now look at the three pictures in that row. What is this selection mostly about? —** *vegetable gardens... farmers markets...grocery stores?* **Circle the picture that shows what the selection is mostly about.**

2. **Move down to the next row. Find the circle. Put your finger on it. Why does the author tell you about fresh eggs? —** *to tell you what you can buy at a farmers market...to share a silly story about an egg...to make you eat eggs?* **Circle the picture that shows why the author told about fresh eggs.**

3. **Move down to the next row. Find the triangle. Put your finger on it. What is going to an outdoor market most like? —** *visiting a farm...going to a baseball game...visiting a park?* **Circle the picture that shows what a farmers market is most like.**

WRITING

On a separate sheet of paper, students will draw a picture of something they might see at a farmers market. Then they will write or dictate something about their drawing. Record the sentences under the picture.

Teacher Scripting: Unit 2 Week 1 Progress Check-Up

HIGH-FREQUENCY WORDS

Turn to page 16. Use the following directions to administer the assessment. Directions in bold are to be read aloud. Students are to respond by circling the answer to each question.

Move through the assessment quickly to make sure you are assessing the student's ability to recognize the high-frequency words.

Look at the first page. I will say a word in each row, and you will circle the word I am saying.

1. **Find the square at the top of the page. Put your finger on the square. Now look at the three words in that row. Draw a circle around the word *are...are.***

2. **Move down to the next row. Find the circle. Put your finger on it. Now look at the three words in that row. Draw a circle around the word *that...that.***

3. **Move down to the next row. Find the triangle. Put your finger on it. Now look at the three words in that row. Draw a circle around the word *of...of.***

PHONICS

Turn to page 17. Move through this assessment a bit more slowly than you did for high-frequency words. The students will need more time to answer these questions.

Turn to the second page. I will tell you the sound a letter makes, and you will circle the picture that has the same sound.

1. **Find the square at the top of the page. Put your finger on it. Now look at the three pictures in that row: *dog...ball...pot*. The letter *d* makes the sound /d/. Draw a circle around the picture that has the beginning *d* sound: *dog...ball...pot.***

2. **Move down to the next row of pictures where you see the circle. Put your finger on it. Now look at the three pictures in that row: *top...kite...bird*. The letter *d* makes the sound /d/. Draw a circle around the picture that has the ending *d* sound: *top... kite...bird.***

3. **Move down to the next row of pictures where you see the triangle. Put your finger on it. Now look at the three pictures in that row: *hat...wall...sock*. The letter *k* makes the sound /k/. Draw a circle around the picture that has the ending *k* sound: *hat... wall...sock.***

4. **Move down to the next row of pictures where you see the heart. Put your finger on it. Now look at the three pictures in that row: *apple...key...door*. The letter *k* makes the /k/ sound. Draw a circle around the picture that has the beginning *k* sound: *apple... key...door.***

LISTENING COMPREHENSION

Turn to page 18. You will read a selection and comprehension questions to the students.

Turn to the last page of your assessment. Now I will read a selection about animals who visit a place called the tundra. Then I will ask you some questions. Listen carefully. Here is the selection.

The Tundra

The tundra is a special place. You will not see many trees here. You will see lots of bushes and grass. In some places, the ground is always frozen. During the winter, the tundra is very cold. There is a lot of snow. It is very quiet in the cold winter. Many animals hibernate, or sleep all through the winter. Many animals leave to go to warmer places.

In the spring, the tundra is filled with noise and activity! As soon as the snow melts, many kinds of animals come back to live in the tundra. The warm weather means there will be many good things to eat. Some animals eat plants. Some animals catch fish in the streams and rivers.

Birds come to the tundra every year. They fly to the tundra from far away. In the springtime, they will build nests and lay eggs.

In spring and summer, there are many new baby animals. In fall, it will be time to move to warmer places. But next spring, the animals will return to the tundra once again.

Now I will ask you some questions about the selection. For each question there are three pictures in a row. Draw a circle around the picture that shows the best answer. Listen carefully.

1. **Find the square at the top of the page and put your finger on it. Now look at the three pictures in that row. What is this selection mostly about?** *trees...winter...the tundra?* **Circle the picture that shows what this selection is mostly about.**

2. **Move down to the next row. Find the circle. Put your finger on it. What do the details in this selection mostly describe?** *the animals...the snow...the rivers?* **Circle the picture that shows what the details in this selection are mostly about.**

3. **Move down to the next row. Find the triangle. Put your finger on it. What is one reason many birds come to the tundra in the spring?** *to fish...to sleep...to build nests?* **Circle the picture that shows why many birds comes to the tundra in the spring.**

WRITING

On a separate sheet of paper, students will draw a picture of an animal. Then they will write or dictate a detail that tells about the animal. Record the detail under the picture.

HIGH-FREQUENCY WORDS

Turn to page 19. Use the following directions to administer the assessment. Directions in bold are to be read aloud. Students are to respond by circling the answer to each question.

Move through the assessment quickly to make sure you are assessing the student's ability to recognize the high-frequency words.

Look at the first page. I will say a word in each row, and you will circle the word I am saying.

1. **Find the square at the top of the page. Put your finger on the square. Now look at the three words in that row. Draw a circle around the word _they...they_.**

2. **Move down to the next row. Find the circle. Put your finger on it. Now look at the three words in that row. Draw a circle around the word _you...you_.**

3. **Move down to the next row. Find the triangle. Put your finger on it. Now look at the three words in that row. Draw a circle around the word _do...do_.**

PHONICS

Turn to page 20. Move through this assessment a bit more slowly than you did for high-frequency words. The students will need more time to answer these questions.

Turn to the second page. I will tell you about the sound a letter makes, and you will circle the picture of the word with that sound.

1. **Find the square at the top of the page. Put your finger on it. Now look at the three pictures in that row: _fly...leaf...mop_. The short _o_ makes the sound /o/. Draw a circle around the picture that has the short _o_ sound: _fly...leaf...mop_.**

2. **Move down to the next row of pictures where you see the circle. Put your finger on it. Now look at the three pictures in that row: _tree...car...rock_. The short _o_ makes the sound /o/. Draw a circle around the picture that has the short _o_ sound: _tree... car...rock_.**

3. **Move down to the next row of pictures where you see the triangle. Put your finger on it. Now look at the three pictures in that row: _fox...wagon...book_. The letter _f_ makes the sound /f/. Draw a circle around the picture that has the beginning _f_ sound: _fox... wagon...book_.**

4. **Move down to the next row of pictures where you see the heart. Put your finger on it. Now look at the three pictures in that row: _cup...fork...bat_. The letter _f_ makes the /f/ sound. Draw a circle around the picture that has the beginning _f_ sound: _cup... fork...bat_.**

LISTENING COMPREHENSION

Turn to page 21. You will read a selection and comprehension questions to the students.

Turn to the last page of your assessment. Now I will read a selection about the different kinds of homes animals live in. Then I will ask you some questions. Listen carefully. Here is the selection.

Where Do Animals Live?

People live in homes. Animals live in homes too. Some animals build their own homes. Others live in homes they find outside.

Many birds build their homes. Some birds build nests high up in trees. Birds might use grass, twigs, or mud to build their nests.

Bears find their homes. They find homes that are good for sleeping in. Bears sleep all winter. Bears live in caves that are dark.

Beavers use things found in nature to build their homes. First, a beaver finds a spot near the water or in the water. Next, it finds sticks, mud, and rocks. Finally, it builds its home.

Some animals build homes in the ground called burrows. Prairie dogs live in burrows. First, a prairie dog digs in the ground. Then, it makes tunnels underground. They keep their food in the tunnels they make underground.

The next time you are outside, take a look around you. Try to spot the places animals live!

Now I will ask you some questions about the selection. For each question, there are three pictures in a row. Draw a circle around the picture that shows the best answer. Listen carefully.

1. **Find the square at the top of the page and put your finger on it. Now look at the three pictures in that row. What must happen first before prairie dogs can keep their food in a tunnel? They must —** *make a burrow...build a nest...be near water?* **Circle the picture that shows what a prairie dog must do first before keeping food in a tunnel.**

2. **Move down to the next row. Find the circle. Put your finger on it. What comes after beavers find a place to live? They —** *go high into a tree...dig a hole...find sticks, mud, and rocks?* **Circle the picture that shows what beavers do after they find a place to live.**

3. **Move down to the next row. Find the triangle. Put your finger on it. What must a bear do first before going to sleep all winter?** *find a cave...look for trees...make a hole in the ground?* **Circle the picture that shows what bears must do first before they go to sleep all winter.**

WRITING

On a separate sheet of paper, students will draw a picture of an animal home. Then they will write or dictate the name of the animal that lives in the home. Record students responses under the picture.

Progress Check-Ups

Teacher Scripting: Unit 2 Week 3 Progress Check-Up

HIGH-FREQUENCY WORDS

Turn to page 22. Use the following directions to administer the assessment. Directions in bold are to be read aloud. Students are to respond by circling the answer to each question.

Move through the assessment quickly to make sure you are assessing the student's ability to recognize the high-frequency words.

Look at the first page. I will say a word in each row, and you will circle the word I am saying.

1. **Find the square at the top of the page. Put your finger on the square. Now look at the three words in that row. Draw a circle around the word *one...one*.**

2. **Move down to the next row. Find the circle. Put your finger on it. Now look at the three words in that row. Draw a circle around the word *two...two*.**

3. **Move down to the next row. Find the triangle. Put your finger on it. Now look at the three words in that row. Draw a circle around the word *three...three*.**

PHONICS

Turn to page 23. Move through this assessment a bit more slowly than you did for high-frequency words. The students will need more time to answer these questions.

Turn to the second page. I will tell you about the sound a letter makes, and you will circle the picture that has the same sound.

1. **Find the square at the top of the page. Put your finger on it. Now look at the three pictures in that row: *hat...dog...bus*. The beginning letter *h* makes the sound /h/. Draw a circle around the picture that has the beginning *h* sound: *hat...dog...bus*.**

2. **Move down to the next row of pictures where you see the circle. Put your finger on it. Now look at the three pictures in that row: *cake...house...sack*. The beginning letter *h* makes the sound /h/. Draw a circle around the picture that has the beginning *h* sound: *cake...house...sack*.**

3. **Move down to the next row of pictures where you see the triangle. Put your finger on it. Now look at the three pictures in that row: *lamp...duck...pen*. The letter *l* makes the sound /l/. Draw a circle around the picture that has the beginning *l* sound: *lamp...duck...pen*.**

4. **Move down to the next row of pictures where you see the heart. Put your finger on it. Now look at the three pictures in that row: *dish...bird...leaf*. The letter *l* makes the sound /l/. Draw a circle around the picture that has the beginning *l* sound: *dish...bird...leaf*.**

LISTENING COMPREHENSION

Turn to page 24. You will read a selection and comprehension questions to the students.

Turn to the last page of your assessment. Now I will read a selection about how a girl decides what to wear to go outside. Then I will ask you some questions. Listen carefully. Here is the selection.

What Shall I Wear?

Rosa looked out the window. A drop of water hit the window! Then, another! It was raining.

"Rosa," said her mother. "It is time for school! You need to get ready to go."

Rosa went to her closet. She pulled down a thick red scarf. Next, she got her favorite blue sweater and started to put it on.

"No, Rosa," said her mother. "That is for when it is very cold outside."

Rosa put the scarf and sweater back. Then she pulled out a bright green straw hat with a pink flower. Rosa always wore this when she helped her mother in the garden.

"No, Rosa," said her mother. "That is for when it is hot and sunny outside."

Rosa put the hat back. She pulled out a yellow rain jacket and a pair of red rain boots. She put them on.

Her mother smiled and said, "Now you are ready!"

"Wait, Mom," said Rosa. She handed her mother an umbrella. Together, they went outside.

Now I will ask you some questions about the selection. For each question there are three pictures in a row. Draw a circle around the picture that shows the best answer. Listen carefully.

1. **Find the square at the top of the page and put your finger on it. Now look at the three pictures in that row. Who are the characters in this story?** *the clothes...the weather outside...Rosa and her mother?* **Circle the picture that shows the characters.**

2. **Move down to the next row. Find the circle. Put your finger on it. What did Rosa finally decide to wear?** *a scarf...a hat...a raincoat?* **Circle the picture that shows what Rosa finally decided to wear.**

3. **Move down to the next row. Find the triangle. Put your finger on it. What does giving her mother an umbrella tell you about Rosa?** *she is excited...she is sad...she is kind?* **Circle the picture that shows what giving her mother the umbrella tells you about Rosa.**

WRITING

On a separate sheet of paper, students will draw a picture of something they like to wear. Then they will write or tell one detail about the thing they like to wear. Record the sentences under the picture.

HIGH-FREQUENCY WORDS

Turn to page 25. Use the following directions to administer the assessment. Directions in bold are to be read aloud. Students are to respond by circling the answer to each question.

Move through the assessment quickly to make sure you are assessing the student's ability to recognize the high-frequency words.

Look at the first page. I will say a word in each row, and you will circle the word I am saying.

1. **Find the square at the top of the page. Put your finger on the square. Now look at the three words in that row. Draw a circle around the word *four...four*.**

2. **Move down to the next row. Find the circle. Put your finger on it. Now look at the three words in that row. Draw a circle around the word *five...five*.**

3. **Move down to the next row. Find the triangle. Put your finger on it. Now look at the three words in that row. Draw a circle around the word *here...here*.**

PHONICS

Turn to page 26. Move through this assessment a bit more slowly than you did for high-frequency words. The students will need more time to answer these questions.

Turn to the second page. I will tell you about the sound a letter makes, and you will circle the picture that has the same sound.

1. **Find the square at the top of the page. Put your finger on it. Now look at the three pictures in that row: *tent...lamb...gate*. The beginning letter *g* makes the sound /g/. Draw a circle around the picture that has the beginning *g* sound: *tent...lamb...gate*.**

2. **Move down to the next row of pictures where you see the circle. Put your finger on it. Now look at the three pictures in that row: *leap...game...bike*. The beginning letter *g* makes the sound /g/. Draw a circle around the picture that has the beginning *g* sound: *leap...game...bike*.**

3. **Move down to the next row of pictures where you see the triangle. Put your finger on it. Now look at the three pictures in that row: *star...cow...lion*. Two consonants together can make the blended sound /st/. Draw a circle around the picture that has the /st/ sound: *star...cow...lion*.**

4. **Move down to the next row of pictures where you see the heart. Put your finger on it. Now look at the three pictures in that row: *bed...draw...pail*. Two consonants together can make the blended sound /dr/. Draw a circle around the picture that has a /dr/ sound: *bed...draw...pail*.**

LISTENING COMPREHENSION

Turn to page 27. You will read a selection and comprehension questions to the students.

Turn to the last page of your assessment. Now I will read a selection about dinosaurs. Then I will ask you some questions. Listen carefully. Here is the selection.

Dinner for Dinosaurs

Long ago, dinosaurs walked the earth. Some were large, and some were small. Some had short tails, and some had long necks. Some dinosaurs ate plants. Others ate meat.

Plant-Eating Dinosaurs

Some dinosaurs liked to eat plants. They ate things like tree branches, leaves, and seeds. Plant-eating dinosaurs had teeth that were big and flat. The shape of their teeth helped them chew plants.

Meat-Eating Dinosaurs

Some dinosaurs were meat-eaters. They ate other dinosaurs, lizards, and turtles. Meat-eating dinosaurs had long, sharp teeth. The shape of their teeth helped them catch and eat their food.

Studying Dinosaurs

Scientists study fossils of dinosaur bones and teeth. They can tell how big dinosaurs were by the size of their bones. They use clues from the teeth to tell what the dinosaurs ate.

Now I will ask you some questions about the selection. For each question there are three pictures in a row. Draw a circle around the picture that shows the best answer. Listen carefully.

1. **Find the square at the top of the page and put your finger on it. Now look at the three pictures in that row. The title of the story tells the reader that the story is about—** *plants...dinosaurs...turtles?* **Circle the picture that shows what the title tells the reader the story is about.**
2. **Move down to the next row. Find the circle. Put your finger on it. Which picture would best help the reader understand the selection?** *dinosaur teeth...leaves... lizards?* **Circle the picture that would best help the reader understand the selection.**
3. **Move down to the next row. Find the triangle. Put your finger on it. Which picture would best help the reader understand how scientists learn about dinosaurs?** *a dinosaur with a long tail...a plant-eating dinosaur...a fossil?* **Circle the picture that would best help the reader understand how scientists learn about dinosaurs.**

WRITING

On a separate sheet of paper, students will draw a picture of an animal. Then they will write or dictate one food they think the animal eats. Record responses under the picture.

Teacher Scripting: Unit 2 Week 5 Progress Check-Up

HIGH-FREQUENCY WORDS

Turn to page 28. Use the following directions to administer the assessment. Directions in bold are to be read aloud. Students are to respond by circling circle the answer to each question.

Move through the assessment quickly to make sure you are assessing the student's ability to recognize the high-frequency words.

Look at the first page. I will say a word in each row, and you will circle the word I am saying.

1. **Find the square at the top of the page. Put your finger on the square. Now look at the three words in that row. Draw a circle around the word *go...go*.**

2. **Move down to the next row. Find the circle. Put your finger on it. Now look at the three words in that row. Draw a circle around the word *from...from*.**

3. **Move down to the next row. Find the triangle. Put your finger on it. Now look at the three words in that row. Draw a circle around the word *yellow...yellow*.**

PHONICS

Turn to page 29. Move through this assessment a bit more slowly than you did for high-frequency words. The students will need more time to answer these questions.

Turn to the second page. I will tell you about the sound a letter makes, and you will circle the picture that has the same sound.

1. **Find the square at the top of the page. Put your finger on it. Now look at the three pictures in that row: *feet...red...weed*. The short *e* makes the sound /e/. Draw a circle around the picture that has the short *e* sound: *feet...red...weed*.**

2. **Move down to the next row of pictures where you see the circle. Put your finger on it. Now look at the three pictures in that row: *meat...beach...ten*. The short *e* makes the sound /e/. Draw a circle around the picture that has the short *e* sound: *meat...beach...ten*.**

3. **Move down to the next row of pictures where you see the triangle. Put your finger on it. Now look at the three pictures in that row: *watch...run...bed*. The letter *w* makes the sound /w/. Draw a circle around the picture that has the beginning *w* sound: *watch...run...bed*.**

4. **Move down to the next row of pictures where you see the heart. Put your finger on it. Now look at the three pictures in that row: *bow...yard...two*. The letter *y* makes the /y/ sound. Draw a circle around the picture that has the beginning *y* sound: *bow...yard...two*.**

Progress Check-Ups

LISTENING COMPREHENSION

Turn to page 30. You will read a selection and comprehension questions to the students.

Turn to the last page of your assessment. Now I will read a selection about jumping rope. Then I will ask you some questions. Listen carefully. Here is the selection.

Everybody Jump!

What is your favorite way to play? My sister likes to ride her bicycle. My brother zooms around on his skateboard. Those things are fun, but jumping rope is the most fun! You can jump rope by yourself, but it is more fun with friends.

One reason I like to jump rope is because there are so many different ways you can play. One of my favorite games is *Jump the Worm*. This is where you have a friend put the rope on the ground. Then, your friend wiggles the rope back and forth like a worm. Now you have to hop over the rope. You don't want the rope to touch you, so you have to be quick.

Jumping rope is good for you, too! My best friend likes to jump rope. We practice our counting when we jump rope. We get plenty of exercise and practice our numbers, too!

My mom says jumping rope is good for you in other ways. It helps keep your heart strong. I like it most of all because it is so much fun. It is the best time ever!

Now I will ask you some questions about the selection. For each question there are three pictures in a row. Draw a circle around the picture that shows the best answer. Listen carefully.

1. **Find the square at the top of the page and put your finger on it. Now look at the three pictures in that row. What does the author say is the most fun? *riding a bike... skateboarding...jumping rope?* Circle the picture that shows what the author says is the most fun.**

2. **Move down to the next row. Find the circle. Put your finger on it. According to the author, what is one good reason to jump rope? *you can hop...you can run...you can practice numbers?* Circle the picture that shows one reason the author likes to jump rope.**

3. **Move down to the next row. Find the triangle. Put your finger on it. What is *Jump the Worm*? *a jump rope game...a way to ride a bike...a skateboard trick?* Circle the picture that shows what *Jump the Worm* is.**

WRITING

On a separate sheet of paper, students will draw a picture of their favorite way to play. Then they will write about or dictate three ways they like to play. Record their responses under the picture.

HIGH-FREQUENCY WORDS

Turn to page 31. Use the following directions to administer the assessment. Directions in bold are to be read aloud. The others are for your information only. Students are to respond by circling the answer to each question.

Move through the assessment quickly to make sure you are assessing the student's ability to recognize the high-frequency words.

Look at the first page. I will say a word in each row, and you will circle the word I am saying.

1. **Find the square at the top of the page. Put your finger on the square. Now look at the three words in that row. Draw a circle around the word *said...said.***

2. **Move down to the next row. Find the circle. Put your finger on it. Now look at the three words in that row. Draw a circle around the word *was...was.***

3. **Move down to the next row. Find the triangle. Put your finger on it. Now look at the three words in that row. Draw a circle around the word *where...where.***

PHONICS

Turn to page 32. Move through this assessment more slowly than you did for high-frequency words. The students will need more time to answer these questions.

Turn to the second page. I will tell you about the sound a letter makes, and you will circle the picture of the word with that sound.

1. **Find the square at the top of the page. Put your finger on it. Now look at the three pictures in that row: *jar...car...dog.* The letter *j* makes the sound /j/. Draw a circle around the picture that has the beginning *j* sound: *jar...car...dog.***

2. **Move down to the next row of pictures where you see the circle. Put your finger on it. Now look at the three pictures in that row: *goat...jacket...tree.* The letter *j* makes the sound /j/. Draw a circle around the picture that has the beginning *j* sound: *goat... jacket...tree.***

3. **Move down to the next row of pictures where you see the triangle. Put your finger on it. Now look at the three pictures in that row: *frog...box...shell.* The letter *x* makes the sound /ks/. Draw a circle around the picture that has the *x* sound: *frog...box... shell.***

4. **Move down to the next row of pictures where you see the heart. Put your finger on it. Now look at the three pictures in that row: *clock...horse...six.* The letter *x* makes the sound /ks/. Draw a circle around the picture that has the *x* sound: *clock...horse...six.***

LISTENING COMPREHENSION

Turn to page 33. You will read a selection and comprehension questions to the students.

Turn to the last page of your assessment. Now I will read a selection about a hero. Then I will ask you some questions. Listen carefully. Here is the selection.

Glooscap the Hero

Many years ago, beavers were much bigger than they are today. This meant that they built very big dams, or walls of branches in the water.

One day, the people noticed that there were no more fish near their village. The beavers had built a dam across the river. The fish could not swim past it. The people were not happy. They liked to fish in that part of the river.

The leaders of the village met. They sent people out in canoes to see if they could break up the dam. But when the canoes got near the beavers, the beavers moved their tails in the water. This made large waves. The canoes could not get close to the dam.

The leaders met again. They asked Glooscap the hero for help. The leaders told him about the problem with the beavers. Glooscap walked right into the river and broke up the dam with his club. Then, he went to the leader of the beavers and picked him up. Glooscap carried the leader many miles away. Then, Glooscap came back to the river. Glooscap saw two beavers and patted each one on the head. As he did this, they became smaller. Soon, all the beavers were the smaller beavers they are today.

Now I will ask you some questions. For each question, there are three pictures in a row. Draw a circle around the picture that shows the best answer. Listen carefully.

1. **Find the square at the top of the page and put your finger on it. Now look at the three pictures in that row. What word best tells how the people feel when the fish could not swim past the dam?** *upset…happy…tired?* **Circle the picture that shows how the people feel.**

2. **Move down to the next row. Find the circle. Put your finger on it. According to the author, what do the leaders do when they cannot break the dam themselves?** *They talk to the beavers…They ask a hero for help…They go fishing?* **Circle the picture that shows what the leaders do when they cannot break the dam.**

3. **Move down to the next row. Find the triangle. Put your finger on it. What is the big idea, or theme, of this story?** *Beavers are smart…Fishing is fun…Sometimes you need help?* **Circle the picture that shows what the author is trying to say.**

WRITING

On a separate sheet of paper, students will draw a picture of the characters and setting in a fiction story they imagine. Then they will write or dictate a sentence telling about an event in the story. Record the sentence under the picture.

Teacher Scripting: Unit 3 Week 2 Progress Check-Up

HIGH-FREQUENCY WORDS

Turn to page 34. Use the following directions to administer the assessment. Directions in bold are to be read aloud. The others are for your information only. Students are to respond by circling the answer to each question.

Move through the assessment quickly to make sure you are assessing the student's ability to recognize the high-frequency words.

Look at the first page. I will say a word in each row, and you will circle the word I am saying.

1. **Find the square at the top of the page. Put your finger on the square. Now look at the three words in that row. Draw a circle around the word** *come...come.*

2. **Move down to the next row. Find the circle. Put your finger on it. Now look at the three words in that row. Draw a circle around the word** *play...play.*

3. **Move down to the next row. Find the triangle. Put your finger on it. Now look at the three words in that row. Draw a circle around the word** *any...any.*

PHONICS

Turn to page 35. Move through this assessment more slowly than you did for high-frequency words. The students will need more time to answer these questions.

Turn to the second page. I will tell you about the sound a letter makes, and you will circle the picture of the word with that sound.

1. **Find the square at the top of the page. Put your finger on it. Now look at the three pictures in that row:** *rug...dog...bird.* **The short** *u* **makes the sound /u/. Draw a circle around the picture that has the short** *u* **sound:** *rug...dog...bird.*

2. **Move down to the next row of pictures where you see the circle. Put your finger on it. Now look at the three pictures in that row:** *mop...hug...sit.* **The short** *u* **makes the sound /u/. Draw a circle around the picture that has the short** *u* **sound:** *mop...hug... sit.*

3. **Move down to the next row of pictures where you see the triangle. Put your finger on it. Now look at the three pictures in that row:** *vase...shell...watch.* **The letter** *v* **makes the sound /v/. Draw a circle around the picture that has the beginning** *v* **sound:** *vase...shell...watch.*

4. **Move down to the next row of pictures where you see the heart. Put your finger on it. Now look at the three pictures in that row:** *cat...water...volcano.* **The letter** *v* **makes the sound /v/. Draw a circle around the picture that has the beginning** *v* **sound:** *cat... water...volcano.*

LISTENING COMPREHENSION

Turn to page 36. You will read a selection and comprehension questions to the students.

Turn to the last page of your assessment. Now I will read two selections about a princess and a prince. Then I will ask you some questions. Listen carefully.

The Princess and the Pea

Once upon a time, a boy met a princess. He wanted to marry her. The boy's mother wanted to make sure the girl was a princess. She went into the guest bedroom. She put a tiny pea under a big pile of mattresses. A princess would feel the pea, even under many mattresses.

The next morning, the boy's mother asked, "How did you sleep?"

"Oh, not very well," said the girl. "I was lying on something hard all night." Then, the boy's mother knew the girl was a true princess.

The Prince and the Sheet

Once upon a time, a prince had been traveling a long time. He came to a house and said, "I am the prince. I am tired. May I sleep here tonight?"

The family who lived in the house was not sure if he was a prince. However, they let him stay. The father said to his daughter, "Put this sheet on the bed in his bedroom. If he says there are too many wrinkles, we will know he is the true prince."

The girl put the sheet on the bed. The next morning, the prince said, "I didn't sleep at all. There were so many wrinkles in the sheet!"

Now I will ask you some questions. For each question, there are three pictures in a row. Draw a circle around the picture that shows the best answer. Listen carefully.

1. **Find the square at the top of the page and put your finger on it. Now look at the three pictures in that row. How is the prince in "The Prince and the Sheet" different from the princess in "The Princess and the Pea"** *he is running…he had been traveling…he is dancing.* **Circle the picture that shows how the prince is different from the princess.**

2. **Move down to the next row. Find the circle. Put your finger on it. How do the prince and the princess feel in the morning?** *tired…happy…surprised.* **Circle the picture that shows how the prince and the princess feel in the morning.**

3. **Move down to the next row. Find the triangle. Put your finger on it. What did the family learn about the man in "The Prince and the Sheet"?** *he works hard…he plans to run away…he is a prince.* **Circle the picture that shows what the family learned about the man.**

WRITING

On a separate sheet of paper, students will think of a story about something that happened to them. They will draw a picture and dictate a list telling what happened. Record the list under the picture.

Teacher Scripting: Unit 3 Week 3 Progress Check-Up

HIGH-FREQUENCY WORDS

Turn to page 37. Use the following directions to administer the assessment. Directions in bold are to be read aloud. The others are for your information only. Students are to respond by circling the answer to each question.

Move through the assessment quickly to make sure you are assessing the student's ability to recognize the high-frequency words.

Look at the first page. I will say a word in each row, and you will circle the word I am saying.

1. **Find the square at the top of the page. Put your finger on the square. Now look at the three words in that row. Draw a circle around the word _down...down._**

2. **Move down to the next row. Find the circle. Put your finger on it. Now look at the three words in that row. Draw a circle around the word _her...her._**

3. **Move down to the next row. Find the triangle. Put your finger on it. Now look at the three words in that row. Draw a circle around the word _how...how._**

PHONICS

Turn to page 38. As you say a word aloud, the student will circle it. Move through this assessment a bit more slowly than you did for high-frequency words. The students will need more time to answer these questions.

Turn to the second page. I will tell you about the sound a letter makes, and you will circle the picture of the word with that sound.

1. **Find the square at the top of the page. Put your finger on it. Now look at the three pictures in that row: _zero...yo-yo...shell._ The letter _z_ makes the sound /z/. Draw a circle around the picture that has the beginning _z_ sound: _zero...yo-yo...shell._**

2. **Move down to the next row of pictures where you see the circle. Put your finger on it. Now look at the three pictures in that row: _shout...zipper...water._ The letter _z_ makes the sound /z/. Draw a circle around the picture that has the beginning _z_ sound: _shout...zipper...water._**

3. **Move down to the next row of pictures where you see the triangle. Put your finger on it. Now look at the three pictures in that row: _barn...quilt...cat._ The letter _q_ makes the sound /kw/. Draw a circle around the picture that has the beginning _q_ sound: _barn...quilt...cat._**

4. **Move down to the next row of pictures where you see the heart. Put your finger on it. Now look at the three pictures in that row: _quarter...hat...car._ The letter _q_ makes the sound /kw/. Draw a circle around the picture that has the beginning _q_ sound: _quarter...hat...car._**

LISTENING COMPREHENSION

Turn to page 39. You will read a selection and comprehension questions to the students.

Turn to the last page of your assessment. Now I will read a selection about a robot. Then I will ask you some questions. Listen carefully. Here is the selection.

Go, Go, Robot!

by Charlotte Gunnufson

With metal fingers and metal toes,
I'm a robot that go-go-goes!
Lift this lever and I will hop!
Push it down and I will stop!
Press my nose: Beep! Beep! Beep!
I'll slow down and creep…creep…creep

Now I will ask you some questions about the selection. For each question that I ask, there are three pictures in a row. Draw a circle around the picture that shows the best answer. Listen carefully.

1. **Find the square at the top of the page and put your finger on it. Now look at the three pictures in that row. Which word is used to rhyme with *goes* in the poem? *toes…robot…fingers.* Circle the picture that rhymes with *goes.***

2. **Move down to the next row. Find the circle. Put your finger on it. What word is used to rhyme with *hop* in the poem? *fingers…nose…stop.* Circle the picture that rhymes with *hop.***

3. **Move down to the next row. Find the triangle. Put your finger on it. What is the robot in this poem mostly doing? *eating…moving…sleeping.* Circle the picture that shows what the robot in this poem is mostly doing.**

WRITING

On a separate sheet of paper, students will draw a picture representing their favorite fiction book, and then write or dictate sentences describing events at the beginning and the end of the book. Record the sentences under the picture.

HIGH-FREQUENCY WORDS

Turn to page 40. Use the following directions to administer the assessment. Directions in bold are to be read aloud. The others are for your information only. Students are to respond by circling the answer to each question.

Move through the assessment quickly to make sure you are assessing the student's ability to recognize the high-frequency words.

Look at the first page. I will say a word in each row, and you will circle the word I am saying.

1. **Find the square at the top of the page. Put your finger on the square. Now look at the three words in that row. Draw a circle around the word *away...away*.**

2. **Move down to the next row. Find the circle. Put your finger on it. Now look at the three words in that row. Draw a circle around the word *give...give*.**

3. **Move down to the next row. Find the triangle. Put your finger on it. Now look at the three words in that row. Draw a circle around the word *little...little*.**

PHONICS

Turn to page 41. Move through this assessment more slowly than you did for high-frequency words. The students will need more time to answer these questions.

Turn to the second page. I will tell you about the sound a letter makes, and you will circle the picture that has the same sound.

1. **Find the square at the top of the page. Put your finger on it. Now look at the three pictures in that row: *cup...hat...date*. The short *a* makes the sound /a/. Draw a circle around the picture that has the short *a* sound: *cup...hat...date*.**

2. **Move down to the next row of pictures where you see the circle. Put your finger on it. Now look at the three pictures in that row: *cat...lake...dog*. The short *a* makes the sound /a/. Draw a circle around the picture that has the short *a* sound: *cat...lake... dog*.**

3. **Move down to the next row of pictures where you see the triangle. Put your finger on it. Now look at the three pictures in that row: *bat...desk...cake*. The long *a* makes the sound /ā/. Draw a circle around the picture that has the long *a* sound: *bat...desk... cake*.**

4. **Move down to the next row of pictures where you see the heart. Put your finger on it. Now look at the three pictures in that row: *ape...cap...mat*. The long *a* makes the sound /ā/. Draw a circle around the picture that has the long *a* sound: *ape... cap...mat*.**

LISTENING COMPREHENSION

Turn to page 42. You will read a selection and comprehension questions to the students.

Turn to the last page of your assessment. Now I will read a selection about telling a story. Then I will ask you some questions. Listen carefully. Here is the selection.

Tell Me a Story!

"Will you tell me a story?" asked Andy.

"Okay," said Andy's big sister, Maya. She opened a book of fairy tales. "How about 'Jack and the Beanstalk'?"

Andy did not seem excited at all.

"Tell me a different story," said Andy.

Maya flipped through the pages. "Here is another one. Long ago…"

But Andy was still not happy.

Maya did not know what to do. She began looking around Andy's room. She saw a picture of him with his soccer ball. He was wearing his favorite red sweater. She had an idea.

"Okay, Andy. Tell me if you have heard this one. Once there was a little boy who loved to play soccer. One day, he found a special red sweater."

"Oh, Maya!" Andy giggled. "I think I am going to really like this story!"

Now I will ask you some questions. For each question, there are pictures in a row. Draw a circle around the picture that shows the best answer. Listen carefully.

1. **Find the square at the top of the page and put your finger on it. Now look at the two pictures in that row. Why did the author write this story?** *to entertain…to inform.* **Circle the picture that shows that why the author wrote it.**

2. **Move down to the next row. Find the circle. Put your finger on it. Which group of words best describes a fun detail from this story?** *Andy likes soccer…. Andy reads to his sister…. Andy likes the stories in the book.* **Circle the picture that best tells a fun detail.**

3. **Move down to the next row. Find the triangle. Put your finger on it. What is this story mainly about?** *playing soccer…spending time outside…telling stories.* **Circle the picture that shows what the story is mainly about.**

WRITING

On a separate sheet of paper, students will draw a picture of a make-believe person and write or dictate a sentence about the person they draw. Record the sentence under the picture.

Teacher Scripting: Unit 3 Week 5 Progress Check-Up

HIGH-FREQUENCY WORDS

Turn to page 43. Use the following directions to administer the assessment. Directions in bold are to be read aloud. The others are for your information only. Students are to respond by circling the answer to each question.

Move through the assessment quickly to make sure you are assessing the student's ability to recognize the high-frequency words.

Look at the first page. I will say a word in each row, and you will circle the word I am saying.

1. **Find the square at the top of the page. Put your finger on the square. Now look at the three words in that row. Draw a circle around the word *funny...funny.***

2. **Move down to the next row. Find the circle. Put your finger on it. Now look at the three words in that row. Draw a circle around the word *were...were.***

3. **Move down to the next row. Find the triangle. Put your finger on it. Now look at the three words in that row. Draw a circle around the word *some...some.***

PHONICS

Turn to page 44. As you say a letter that a sound makes, the student will circle a word that has the same sound. Move through this assessment a bit more slowly than you did for high-frequency words. The students will need more time to answer these questions.

Turn to the second page. I will tell you about the sound a letter makes, and you will circle the picture that has the same sound.

1. **Find the square at the top of the page. Put your finger on it. Now look at the three pictures in that row: *mitt...pipe...head.* The long *i* makes the sound /ī/. Draw a circle around the picture that has the long *i* sound: *mitt...pipe...head.***

2. **Move down to the next row of pictures where you see the circle. Put your finger on it. Now look at the three pictures in that row: *pine...park...pin.* The long *i* makes the sound /ī/. Draw a circle around the picture that has the long *i* sound: *pine...park... pin.***

3. **Move down to the next row of pictures where you see the triangle. Put your finger on it. Now look at the three pictures in that row: *kite...bin...rake.* The short *i* makes the sound /i/. Draw a circle around the picture that has the short *i* sound: *kite...bin...rake.***

4. **Move down to the next row of pictures where you see the heart. Put your finger on it. Now look at the three pictures in that row: *stick...ice...hen.* The short *i* makes the sound /i/. Draw a circle around the picture that has the short *i* sound: *stick...ice... hen.***

LISTENING COMPREHENSION

Turn to page 45. You will read a selection to the students.

Turn to the last page of your assessment. Now I will read a selection. Then I will ask you some questions. Listen carefully. Here is the selection.

Pegasus

Long ago, a horse named Pegasus was born. Pegasus was not like any other horse. Pegasus could fly. One day, Pegasus met a brave man.

"I need your help," the man said. "Can I fly with you if I am in danger?"

Pegasus was a good horse. He agreed to help the brave man. Pegasus helped the brave man stay safe. "I am strong like the rulers," said the brave man. "I should be allowed to live with them." He asked Pegasus to carry him up to the land of the rulers.

Pegasus began to fly, but the rulers had heard the brave man. They did not want the brave man to live with them. Zeus, the leader, made a plan. He sent a horsefly to bite Pegasus. Pegasus felt the bite and pawed the air. The brave man lost his balance. He fell off Pegasus and went back to his own land.

Zeus called to Pegasus. "I know you are a loyal horse," he said. "Come live with me. You can help me carry thunder and lightning through the sky."

Pegasus liked this idea and went to live with Zeus. They became good friends.

Now I will ask you some questions about the selection. For each question that I ask, there are three pictures in a row. Draw a circle around the picture that shows the best answer. Listen carefully.

1. **Find the square at the top of the page and put your finger on it. Now look at the three pictures in that row. What happened at the beginning of the story? Pegasus — *was born...was bitten by a fly...lived with Zeus*. Circle the picture that shows what happened at the beginning of the story.**

2. **Move down to the next row. Find the circle. Put your finger on it. What happened in the middle of the story? Pegasus — *was born...lived with Zeus...was bitten by a fly*. Circle the picture that shows what happened in the middle of the story.**

3. **Move down to the next row. Find the triangle. Put your finger on it. What happened at the end of the story? *Pegasus — was bitten by a fly...lived with Zeus...was born*. Circle the picture that shows what happened at the end of the story.**

WRITING

On a separate sheet of paper, students will draw a picture of Pegasus. Then they will dictate a sentence about something Pegasus could do. Record the sentence under the picture.

Teacher Scripting: Unit 4 Week 1 Progress Check-Up

HIGH-FREQUENCY WORDS

Turn to page 46. Use the following directions to administer the assessment. Directions in bold are to be read aloud. Students are to respond by circling the answer to each question.

Move through the assessment quickly to make sure you are assessing the student's ability to recognize the high-frequency words.

Look at the first page. I will say a word in each row, and you will circle the word I am saying.

1. **Find the square at the top of the page. Put your finger on the square. Now look at the three words in that row. Draw a circle around the word** *find...find.*

2. **Move down to the next row. Find the circle. Put your finger on it. Now look at the three words in that row. Draw a circle around the word** *over...over.*

3. **Move down to the next row. Find the triangle. Put your finger on it. Now look at the three words in that row. Draw a circle around the word** *again...again.*

PHONICS

Turn to page 47. Move through this section more slowly than you did for high-frequency words. The students will need more time to answer these questions.

Turn to the second page. I will tell you about the sound a letter makes, and you will circle the picture of the word with that sound.

1. **Find the square at the top of the page. Put your finger on it. Now look at the three pictures in that row:** *rope...stop...pole.* **The short** *o* **makes the sound /o/. Draw a circle around the picture that has the short** *o* **sound:** *rope...stop...pole.*

2. **Move down to the next row of pictures where you see the circle. Put your finger on it. Now look at the three pictures in that row:** *fox...home...phone.* **The short** *o* **makes the sound /o/. Draw a circle around the picture that has the short** *o* **sound:** *fox... home...phone.*

3. **Move down to the next row of pictures where you see the triangle. Put your finger on it. Now look at the three pictures in that row:** *dog...shop...hole.* **The long** *o* **makes the sound /ō/. Draw a circle around the picture that has the long** *o* **sound:** *dog... shop...hole.*

4. **Move down to the next row of pictures where you see the heart. Put your finger on it. Now look at the three pictures in that row:** *mop...nose...doll.* **The long** *o* **makes the sound /ō/. Draw a circle around the picture that has the long** *o* **sound:** *mop...nose...doll.*

LISTENING COMPREHENSION

Turn to page 48. You will read a selection and comprehension questions to the students.

Turn to the last page of your assessment. Now I will read a selection about crayons. Then I will ask you some questions. Listen carefully. Here is the selection.

The Story of Crayons

Do you like to color? You might love opening a new box of crayons. You might love to look at all the colors.

Did you know that crayons were not always so colorful? Hundreds of years ago, all crayons were black.

Early crayons were made by mixing together two black substances—oil and charcoal. This is how they got their black color. Oil and charcoal are also soft and slippery. So, the crayons could get messy. Using them was like using wet chalk to draw.

Color crayons were made starting in the 1800s. Crayon makers began using powder instead of charcoal. The powder could be made in different colors, but the crayons were still messy. So, crayon makers started using wax instead of oil. This made crayons strong and easy to hold. They were a lot less messy!

At first, crayons were used by businesses. Two cousins started mixing safe powders and wax. They created the first box of crayons for children. Each box came with eight colors and cost five cents.

Now I will ask you some questions about the selection. For each question, there are three pictures in a row. Draw a circle around the picture that shows the best answer. Listen carefully.

1. **Find the square at the top of the page and put your finger on it. Now look at the three pictures in that row. The first crayons were made with charcoal and oil and were all what color?** *black...red...white.* **Circle the picture that shows what color the first crayons were.**

2. **Move down to the next row. Find the circle. Put your finger on it. What picture best shows who first used crayons?** *teachers...businesses...children.* **Circle the picture that shows who first used crayons.**

3. **Move down to the next row. Find the triangle. Put your finger on it. Which is the most important difference between the crayons from long ago and crayons used today?** *they are now sold in boxes of five...there are now more colors...the crayons are now all black.* **Circle the picture that shows the important difference between crayons from long ago and crayons today.**

WRITING

On a separate sheet of paper, students will draw a picture with crayons of what they most like drawing and then dictate a sentence that tells about that topic. Students should use and tell about their favorite color. Record the sentences under the picture.

Progress Check-Ups

Teacher Scripting: Unit 4 Week 2 Progress Check-Up

HIGH-FREQUENCY WORDS

Turn to page 49. Use the following directions to administer the assessment. Directions in bold are to be read aloud. Students are to respond by circling the answer to each question.

Move through the assessment quickly to make sure you are assessing the student's ability to recognize the high-frequency words.

Look at the first page. I will say a word in each row, and you will circle the word I am saying.

1. **Find the square at the top of the page. Put your finger on the square. Now look at the three words in that row. Draw a circle around the word *all...all.***

2. **Move down to the next row. Find the circle. Put your finger on it. Now look at the three words in that row. Draw a circle around the word *now...now.***

3. **Move down to the next row. Find the triangle. Put your finger on it. Now look at the three words in that row. Draw a circle around the word *pretty...pretty.***

PHONICS

Turn to page 50. Move through this assessment more slowly than you did for high-frequency words. The students will need more time to answer these questions.

Turn to the second page. I will tell you about the sound a letter makes, and you will circle the picture of the word with that sound.

1. **Find the square at the top of the page. Put your finger on it. Now look at the three pictures in that row: *rug...cube...uniform.* The short *u* makes the sound /u/. Draw a circle around the picture that has the short *u* sound: *rug...cube...uniform.***

2. **Move down to the next row of pictures where you see the circle. Put your finger on it. Now look at the three pictures in that row: *umbrella...ruler...music.* The short *u* makes the sound /u/. Draw a circle around the picture that has the short *u* sound: *umbrella... ruler...music.***

3. **Move down to the next row of pictures where you see the triangle. Put your finger on it. Now look at the three pictures in that row: *tub...flute...cup.* The long *u* makes the sound /ū/. Draw a circle around the picture that has the long *u* sound: *tub...flute...cup.***

4. **Move down to the next row of pictures where you see the heart. Put your finger on it. Now look at the three pictures in that row: *mug...student...nut.* The long *u* makes the sound /ū/. Draw a circle around the picture that has the long *u* sound: *mug... student...nut.***

Progress Check-Ups

LISTENING COMPREHENSION

Turn to page 51. You will read a selection and comprehension questions to the students.

Turn to the last page of your assessment. Now I will read a selection about a time capsule. Then I will ask you some questions. Listen carefully. Here is the selection.

Texas Time Capsule

April 16, 2017, is a day I will never forget. I watched school workers open two time capsules at the University of Texas.

A time capsule is a container that holds items. People collect the items from a year or time period. These items are placed into the time capsule. The capsules are put in a safe place or buried in the ground for a long time. One day in the future, they will be opened.

Time capsules help people learn about the past. The time capsules I saw were from two different years. The first capsule was from 1962. The capsule had books from 1962. It had copies of newspapers written by students. The capsule also had a recording of a speech made by the college president back in 1962!

The second time capsule came from 1988. There was a video made by the college president. The capsule had a picture of a band from the school. It had books from the 1980s. There were also copies of newspapers written by students.

People can still see these items. It is a great way to learn what life was like in 1962 and 1988.

Now I will ask you some questions about the selection. For each question, there are three pictures in a row. Draw a circle around the picture that shows the best answer. Listen carefully.

1. **Find the square at the top of the page and put your finger on it. Now look at the three pictures in that row. What is this selection mostly about?** *a time capsule…going to school…reading newspapers.* **Circle the picture that shows what this selection is mostly about.**

2. **Move down to the next row. Find the circle. Put your finger on it. What picture best shows items found in both time capsules?** *clothing…photographs…books.* **Circle the picture that shows what items were found in both time capsules.**

3. **Move down to the next row. Find the triangle. Put your finger on it. What would you learn the most about from the items in these time capsules?** *school life…home life… farm life.* **Circle the picture that shows what you would learn the most about from the items in the time capsules.**

WRITING

On a separate sheet of paper, students will draw a picture of a favorite place, and then write or dictate a sentence that tells about the place. Record the sentence under the picture.

Teacher Scripting: Unit 4 Week 3 Progress Check-Up

HIGH-FREQUENCY WORDS

Turn to page 52. Use the following directions to administer the assessment. Directions in bold are to be read aloud. Students are to respond by circling the answer to each question.

Move through the assessment quickly to make sure you are assessing the student's ability to recognize the high-frequency words.

Look at the first page. I will say a word in each row, and you will circle the word I am saying.

1. **Find the square at the top of the page. Put your finger on the square. Now look at the three words in that row. Draw a circle around the word *black…black.***

2. **Move down to the next row. Find the circle. Put your finger on it. Now look at the three words in that row. Draw a circle around the word *brown…brown.***

3. **Move down to the next row. Find the triangle. Put your finger on it. Now look at the three words in that row. Draw a circle around the word *white…white.***

PHONICS

Turn to page 53. Move through this assessment more slowly than you did for the high-frequency words. The students will need more time to answer these questions.

Turn to the second page. I will tell you about the sound a letter makes, and you will circle the picture of the word with that sound.

1. **Find the square at the top of the page. Put your finger on it. Now look at the three pictures in that row: *sleeve…bed…bees.* The short *e* makes the sound /e/. Draw a circle around the picture that has the short *e* sound: *sleeve…bed…bees.***

2. **Move down to the next row of pictures where you see the circle. Put your finger on it. Now look at the three pictures in that row: *net…peas…evening.* The short *e* makes the sound /e/. Draw a circle around the picture that has the short *e* sound: *net…peas…evening.***

3. **Move down to the next row of pictures where you see the triangle. Put your finger on it. Now look at the three pictures in that row: *beans…men…sled.* The long *e* makes the sound /ē/. Draw a circle around the picture that has the long *e* sound: *beans…men…sled.***

4. **Move down to the next row of pictures where you see the heart. Put your finger on it. Now look at the three pictures in that row: *egg…melt…feet.* The long *e* makes the sound /ē/. Draw a circle around the picture that has the long *e* sound: *egg…melt…feet.***

LISTENING COMPREHENSION

Turn to page 54. You will read a selection and comprehension questions to the students.

Turn to the last page of your assessment. Now I will read a selection about writing a letter.

Then I will ask you some questions. Listen carefully. Here is the selection.

Grandma's Letter

Chika walked into the living room. Her grandmother was sitting at the desk. "Hi, Grandma, what are you doing?" Chika asked.

"I am writing a letter to my friend Keiko. She lives in Japan," her grandmother replied.

Chika looked at her grandmother. She noticed the careful letters in blue ink printed on the paper. "How is it going to get there?" asked Chika.

**Chika's grandmother smiled. "After I write the letter, I will put it in an envelope. I will write the address on the envelope. Then, I'll attach a stamp to the envelope and put it in the mailbox," she explained. Chika's grandmother pointed to the mailbox at the end of the driveway. "In about a week, it will arrive in Japan."
Chika nodded. "Would it be easier to just send an email?"**

Chika explained that typing was quicker than writing with a pen. Then all she would have to do was type in Keiko's email address. She could send it to Japan very quickly.

"Yes, it is faster," her grandmother replied. "But I like to handwrite a letter. It shows my friends that I wanted to take time to think about them."

Now I will ask you some questions about the selection. For each question, there are three pictures in a row. Draw a circle around the picture that shows the best answer. Listen carefully.

1. **Find the square at the top of the page and put your finger on it. Now look at the three pictures in that row. Where does the story take place?** *in the living room...in the kitchen...in the garden.* **Circle the picture that shows where the story takes place.**

2. **Move down to the next row. Find the circle. Put your finger on it. Where is Chika's grandmother in the story?** *at the kitchen table...at a desk...in the car.* **Circle the picture that shows where Chika's grandmother is in the story.**

3. **Move down to the next row. Find the triangle. Put your finger on it. Where will Chika's grandmother go when she finishes her letter?** *to the store...to the garden... to the mailbox.* **Circle the picture that shows where Chika's grandmother will go after finishing her letter.**

WRITING

On a separate sheet of paper, students will draw a picture of a problem and how they solved it, and then write or dictate about the steps they took to solve the problem. Record what students write or dictate under the picture.

Teacher Scripting: Unit 4 Week 4 Progress Check-Up

HIGH-FREQUENCY WORDS

Turn to page 55. Use the following directions to administer the assessment. Directions in bold are to be read aloud. Students are to respond by circling the answer to each question.

Move through the assessment quickly to make sure you are assessing the student's ability to recognize the high-frequency words.

Look at the first page. I will say a word in each row, and you will circle the word I am saying.

1. **Find the square at the top of the page. Put your finger on the square. Now look at the three words in that row. Draw a circle around the word *good...good.***

2. **Move down to the next row. Find the circle. Put your finger on it. Now look at the three words in that row. Draw a circle around the word *open...open.***

3. **Move down to the next row. Find the triangle. Put your finger on it. Now look at the three words in that row. Draw a circle around the word *could...could.***

PHONICS

Turn to page 56. Move through this assessment more slowly than you did for the high-frequency words. The students will need more time to answer these questions.

Turn to the second page. I will tell you about the sound a letter makes, and you are going to circle the picture of the word with that sound.

1. **Find the square at the top of the page. Put your finger on it. Now look at the three pictures in that row: *pencil...desk...coat.* The letter *p* makes the sound /p/. Draw a circle around the picture that has the /p/ sound: *pencil...desk...coat.***

2. **Move down to the next row of pictures where you see the circle. Put your finger on it. Now look at the three pictures in that row: *gate...yard...rabbit.* The letter *y* makes the sound /y/. Draw a circle around the picture that has the /y/ sound: *gate...yard... rabbit.***

3. **Move down to the next row of pictures where you see the triangle. Put your finger on it. Now look at the three pictures in that row: *ladder...moon...fish.* The short *i* makes the /i/ sound. Draw a circle around the picture that has the /i/ sound: *ladder... moon...fish.***

4. **Move down to the next row of pictures where you see the heart. Put your finger on it. Now look at the three pictures in that row: *dime...door...nail.* The long *i* makes the /ī/ sound. Draw a circle around the picture that has the /ī/ sound: *dime...door...nail.***

LISTENING COMPREHENSION

Turn to page 57. You will read a selection and comprehension questions to the students.

Turn to the last page of your assessment. Now I will read about Katherine Johnson, who helped send people into space. Then I will ask you some questions. Listen carefully. Here is the selection.

The Girl Who Loved Numbers

Katherine Johnson always loved math. She grew up in the 1920s. As a girl, she always thought about numbers. She could not get enough of numbers and counting.

A Love of Learning

Katherine also loved school. She was so good at school that she began high school when she was 10. She continued to learn a lot. Katherine graduated from high school when she was 14. She graduated from college when she was 18. That is when most students start college. Katherine became a teacher. Yet, she still loved numbers. So, in 1953, she began working for a science group.

A Love of Space

Over time, the science group became known as NASA. They were interested in sending people into space. Katherine could help. She used math to figure out paths that rockets should take in space.

This time line shows dates in Katherine life. Let's read it together. (To the Teacher: Draw the time line on the board.)

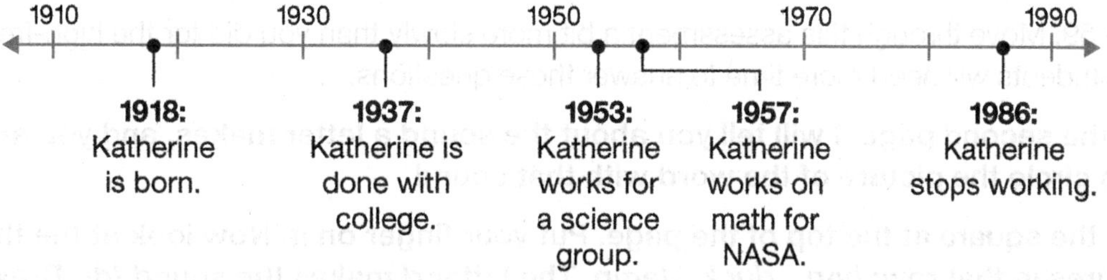

Now I will ask you some questions. For each question, there are three pictures in a row. Draw a circle around the picture that shows the best answer. Listen carefully.

1. Find the square at the top of the page and put your finger on it. Now look at the three pictures in that row. The section titled "A Love of Learning" tells about Katherine Johnson's — *home life…school life…hobbies?* Circle the picture that shows what the section titled "A Love of Learning" tells about Katherine Johnson.

2. Move down to the next row. Find the circle. Put your finger on it. Where would I find information about the date when Katherine Johnson was born? *the time line…the story…the title.* Circle the picture that shows where I would find information about the date when Katherine Johnson was born.

3. Move down to the next row. Find the triangle. Put your finger on it. Why did the author include a time line in the story? *to learn about important dates…to learn more about numbers…to learn about space.* Circle the picture that shows why the author included a time line with the story.

WRITING

On a separate sheet of paper, students will draw and write about something they would like to do when they grow up. Record what students write or dictate under the picture.

Teacher Scripting: Unit 4 Week 5 Progress Check-Up

HIGH-FREQUENCY WORDS

Turn to page 58. Use the following directions to administer the assessment. Directions in bold are to be read aloud. Students are to respond by circling the answer to each question.

Move through the assessment quickly to make sure you are assessing the student's ability to recognize the high-frequency words.

Look at the first page. I will say a word in each row, and you will circle the word I am saying.

1. **Find the square at the top of the page. Put your finger on the square. Now look at the three words in that row. Draw a circle around the word** *please...please.*

2. **Move down to the next row. Find the circle. Put your finger on it. Now look at the three words in that row. Draw a circle around the word** *want...want.*

3. **Move down to the next row. Find the triangle. Put your finger on it. Now look at the three words in that row. Draw a circle around the word** *every...every.*

PHONICS

Turn to page 59. Move through this assessment a bit more slowly than you did for the high-frequency words. The students will need more time to answer these questions.

Turn to the second page. I will tell you about the sound a letter makes, and you are going to circle the picture of the word with that sound.

1. **Find the square at the top of the page. Put your finger on it. Now look at the three pictures in that row:** *hop...duck...lamp.* **The letter** *d* **makes the sound /d/. Draw a circle around the picture that has the sound of the letter** *d: hop...duck...lamp.*

2. **Move down to the next row of pictures where you see the circle. Put your finger on it. Now look at the three pictures in that row:** *rain...father...pail.* **The letter** *f* **makes the sound /f/. Draw a circle around the picture that has the sound of the letter** *f: rain...father...pail.*

3. **Move down to the next row of pictures where you see the triangle. Put your finger on it. Now look at the three pictures in that row:** *clouds...horse...vegetables.* **The letter** *v* **makes the sound /v/. Draw a circle around the picture that has the sound of the letter** *v: clouds...horse...vegetables.*

4. **Move down to the next row of pictures where you see the heart. Put your finger on it. Now look at the three pictures in that row:** *nest...bean...tree.* **The short** *e* **makes the sound /ĕ/. Draw a circle around the picture that has the short** *e* **sound:** *nest...bean...tree.*

LISTENING COMPREHENSION

Turn to page 60. You will read a selection and comprehension questions to the students.

Turn to the last page of your assessment. Now I will read about a boy learning to do a special dance. Then I will ask you some questions. Listen carefully. Here is the selection.

Jonathan's Hoop Dance

"Grandpa, were you as nervous as I am when you first did the hoop dance?" Jonathan asked his grandfather, Henry Red Cloud.

"Oh, I remember being very nervous when my father showed me," Grandpa replied. "However, practice always makes perfect."

"Can you show me one more time how to do it?" Jonathan asked. Jonathan had seen members of other Algonquin family groups perform the hoop dance. It was fast. The dancers moved a lot. This would be the first time Jonathan would join others dancing.

"Sure," Grandpa replied. He took four brightly colored hoops. He placed two over his right arm. He placed the other two over his left arm. "Now watch what I do. You only have to use a few hoops."

Grandpa moved his arms quickly. The hoops moved in circles. Grandpa was able to make different patterns with the hoops as he sped them up and slowed them down. "Imagine you are telling a story as you dance."

Jonathan gave it a try. He tried to copy what Grandpa did. It took a couple of minutes. But soon the hoops were whirling about his arms and legs.

"That is a wonderful story," Grandpa said. "You are going to do great tonight. I cannot wait to see it."

Now I will ask you some questions. For each question, there are three pictures in a row. Draw a circle around the picture that shows the best answer. Listen carefully.

1. Find the square at the top of the page and put your finger on it. Now look at the three pictures in that row. What is this story mainly about? *learning to dance… counting the hoops…playing a game.* Circle the picture that shows what the story is mainly about.

2. Move down to the next row. Find the circle. Put your finger on it. How does Jonathan learn about the tradition of the hoop dance? *from his grandfather…from his brother…from his teacher.* Circle the picture that shows how Jonathan learns about the tradition of the hoop dance.

3. Move down to the next row. Find the triangle. Put your finger on it. How can you tell that the hoop dance is an important tradition to Jonathan's family? *the men teach the boys about the dance…they read about the dance…they watch a movie about the dance.* Circle the picture that shows how you can tell that the hoop dance is an important tradition to Jonathan's family.

WRITING

On a separate sheet of paper, students will draw a picture of a tradition they have with their families. Then they will write or dictate two sentences that tell about it, making sure any names are capitalized. Record the sentences under the picture.

Teacher Scripting: Unit 5 Week 1 Progress Check-Up

HIGH-FREQUENCY WORDS

Turn to page 61. Use the following directions to administer the assessment. Directions in bold are to be read aloud. Students are to respond by circling the answer to each question.

Move through the assessment quickly to make sure you are assessing the student's ability to recognize the high-frequency words.

Look at the first page. I will say a word in each row, and you will circle the word I am saying.

1. **Find the square at the top of the page. Put your finger on the square. Now look at the three words in that row. Draw a circle around the word *be...be.***

2. **Move down to the next row. Find the circle. Put your finger on it. Now look at the three words in that row. Draw a circle around the word *saw...saw.***

3. **Move down to the next row. Find the triangle. Put your finger on it. Now look at the three words in that row. Draw a circle around the word *our...our.***

PHONICS

Turn to page 62. Move through this assessment more slowly than you did for high-frequency words. Students will need more time to answer these questions.

Turn to the second page. I will tell you the sound a letter makes, and you will circle the picture that has the same sound.

1. **Find the square at the top of the page. Put your finger on it. Now look at the three pictures in that row: *gate...pan...cat.* The letter c makes the sound /k/. Draw a circle around the picture that has the sound of the letter *c: gate...pan...cat.***

2. **Move down to the next row where you see the circle. Put your finger on it. Now look at the three pictures in that row: *run...sit...jump.* The letter t makes the sound /t/. Draw a circle around the picture that ends with the sound of the letter *t: run...sit... jump.***

3. **Move down to the next row where you see the triangle. Put your finger on it. Now look at the three pictures in that row: *tie...bone...apple.* The long o makes the sound /ō/. Draw a circle around the picture that has the sound of long *o: tie...bone...apple.***

4. **Move down to the next row where you see the heart. Put your finger on it. Now look at the three pictures in that row: *mop...bug...ice.* The short o makes the sound /ŏ/. Draw a circle around the picture that has the sound of short *o: mop...bug...ice.***

LISTENING COMPREHENSION

Turn to page 63. You will read a selection and comprehension questions to students.

Turn to the last page of your assessment. Now I will read a selection. Then I will ask you some questions. Listen carefully.

A Strange Winter

You know about winter. You know it gets colder. In some places, there is a lot of snow. Did you know that sometimes the ocean can change winter?

Weather and the Ocean

The ocean is very important in our weather. So is the wind. The temperature of the water—that is, how cold or warm the water is—can change winter weather. Strong winds also help to push the warmer waters in different directions.

Rain or Snow?

How does the ocean change winter? If the ocean water becomes warmer, more clouds form. That means more rain will fall.

When the ocean is warmer, the winter will be warmer. Places that usually get snow will have rain instead. Places that are usually dry will get a lot of rain.

Some years the winter weather is strange!

Now I will ask you some questions about the selection. For each question, there are three pictures in a row. Draw a circle around the picture that shows the best answer. Listen carefully.

1. **Find the square at the top of the page and put your finger on it. Now look at the three pictures in that row. Which picture best shows you what the selection is mostly about?** *the ocean...winter weather...rain.* **Circle the picture that shows what the selection is mostly about.**

2. **Move down to the next row. Find the circle. Put your finger on it. Which picture shows what happens when the ocean becomes warmer in winter?** *it rains more... it snows more...it becomes very dry?* **Circle the picture that shows what happens when the ocean becomes warmer in winter.**

3. **Move down to the next row. Find the triangle. Put your finger on it. What might happen if the ocean water stays cold?** *more rain will fall...it will be more windy...the winter will be colder.* **Circle the picture that shows what might happen if the ocean water stays cold.**

WRITING

Students should draw a picture of a weather event such as a thunderstorm. Then, students should write or tell a question and an answer about that weather event. Record each student's question and answer under their picture.

HIGH-FREQUENCY WORDS

Turn to page 64. Use the following directions to administer the assessment. Directions in bold are to be read aloud. Students are to respond by circling the answer to each question.

Move through the assessment quickly to make sure you are assessing the student's ability to recognize the high-frequency words.

Look at the first page. I will say a word in each row, and you will circle the word I am saying.

1. **Find the square at the top of the page. Put your finger on the square. Now look at the three words in that row. Draw a circle around the word *eat...eat*.**

2. **Move down to the next row. Find the circle. Put your finger on it. Now look at the three words in that row. Draw a circle around the word *soon...soon*.**

3. **Move down to the next row. Find the triangle. Put your finger on it. Now look at the three words in that row. Draw a circle around the word *walk...walk*.**

PHONICS

Turn to page 65. Move through this assessment more slowly than you did for high-frequency words. Students will need more time to answer these questions.

Turn to the second page. I will tell you the sound a letter or pair of letters makes, and you will circle the picture that has the same sound.

1. **Find the square at the top of the page. Put your finger on it. Now look at the three pictures in that row: *door...bat...socks*. The letter *b* makes the sound /b/. Draw a circle around the picture that has the sound of the letter *b: door...bat...socks*.**

2. **Move down to the next row where you see the circle. Put your finger on it. Now look at the three pictures in that row: *jar...book...hat*. The letter *j* makes the sound /j/. Draw a circle around the picture that has the sound of the letter *j: jar...book...hat*.**

3. **Move down to the next row where you see the triangle. Put your finger on it. Now look at the three pictures in that row: *sled...lamb...drum*. The letters *sl* make the sound /sl/. Draw a circle around the picture that has the sound of the letters *sl: sled...lamb...drum*.**

4. **Move down to the next row where you see the heart. Put your finger on it. Now look at the three pictures in that row: *girl...camp...lion*. The letters *mp* make the /mp/ sound. Draw a circle around the picture that has the sound of the letters *mp: girl...camp...lion*.**

LISTENING COMPREHENSION

Turn to page 66. You will read a selection and comprehension questions to students.

Turn to the last page of your assessment. Now I will read a selection. Then I will ask you some questions. Listen carefully.

A Tree Changes

You can put on a coat in the winter. You can go inside where it is warm. A tree cannot do these things. A tree needs to do other things when the weather changes.

In the fall, the weather gets cooler. The leaves fall off the tree. Next, the winter comes. There is less light. The tree goes to sleep. The tree has stopped growing now.

When spring arrives, it gets warmer. There is more light. The snow melts away. Now, the tree starts to grow again. You can see buds. Buds are small blossoms and small leaves that appear on the tree branches. Soon the buds will grow into new flowers and new leaves. By summer, the tree is full and green. When fall comes, the tree will lose its leaves. Then, in winter, it will stop growing again.

Now I will ask you some questions about the selection. For each question, there are three pictures in a row. Draw a circle around the picture that shows the best answer. Listen carefully.

1. **Find the square at the top of the page and put your finger on it. Now look at the three pictures in that row. What happens to a tree just before winter comes?** *it sleeps...it loses leaves...it gets buds.* **Circle the picture that shows what happens to a tree just before winter comes.**

2. **Move down to the next row. Find the circle. Put your finger on it. What happens to help the tree during spring?** *there is more snow...there is more darkness...there is more light.* **Circle the picture that shows what happens to help the tree during spring.**

3. **Move down to the next row. Find the triangle. Put your finger on it. What happens to the buds on a tree in the spring?** *they turn into flowers and leaves...they turn into fruit...they make a new tree.* **Circle the picture that shows what happens to buds on a tree in the spring.**

WRITING

Students should draw a picture of what a tree might look like during one of the seasons. For example, students could draw a tree with leaves changing colors in the fall. Then, students should write or tell a complete sentence about the tree that they drew. Record each student's answer under their picture.

HIGH-FREQUENCY WORDS

Turn to page 67. Use the following directions to administer the assessment. Directions in bold are to be read aloud. Students are to respond by circling the answer to each question.

Move through the assessment quickly to make sure you are assessing the student's ability to recognize the high-frequency words.

Look at the first page. I will say a word in each row, and you will circle the word I am saying.

1. **Find the square at the top of the page. Put your finger on the square. Now look at the three words in that row. Draw a circle around the word** *who...who.*

2. **Move down to the next row. Find the circle. Put your finger on it. Now look at the three words in that row. Draw a circle around the word** *into...into.*

3. **Move down to the next row. Find the triangle. Put your finger on it. Now look at the three words in that row. Draw a circle around the word** *there...there.*

PHONICS

Turn to page 68. Move through this assessment more slowly than you did for high-frequency words. Students will need more time to answer these questions.

Turn to the second page. I will tell you the sound a letter makes, and you will circle the picture that has the same sound.

1. **Find the square at the top of the page. Put your finger on it. Now look at the three pictures in that row:** *car...goat...mouse.* **The letter** *g* **makes the sound /g/. Draw a circle around the picture that has the sound of the letter** *g: car...goat...mouse.*

2. **Move down to the next row where you see the circle. Put your finger on it. Now look at the three pictures in that row:** *fin...quiet...ring.* **The letters** *qu* **make the sound /kw/. Draw a circle around the picture that has the sound of the letters** *qu: fin... quiet...ring.*

3. **Move down to the next row where you see the triangle. Put your finger on it. Now look at the three pictures in that row:** *lake...truck...map.* **The short** *a* **makes the sound /a/. Draw a circle around the picture that has the sound of short** *a: lake... truck...map.*

4. **Move down to the next row where you see the heart. Put your finger on it. Now look at the three pictures in that row:** *fox...bake...hook.* **The long** *a* **makes the sound /ā/. Draw a circle around the picture that has the sound of long** *a: fox...bake...hook.*

LISTENING COMPREHENSION

Turn to page 69. You will read a selection and comprehension questions to students.

Turn to the last page of your assessment. Now I will read a selection. Then I will ask you some questions. Listen carefully.

Rainy Day

**The rain falls
From the sky.
It makes puddles
That I spy.**

**The puddles grow
In a flash.
I jump in
With a SPLASH!**

**Sending mud
Here and there.
I jump again
Without a care.**

**When it rains
I love to play.
I wish it'd rain
Every day.**

Now I will ask you some questions. For each question, there are three pictures in a row. Draw a circle around the picture that shows the best answer. Listen carefully.

1. **Find the square at the top of the page and put your finger on it. Now look at the three pictures in that row. What word rhymes with** *spy? rain...falls...sky.* **Circle the picture that shows the word that rhymes with** *spy.*

2. **Move down to the next row. Find the circle. Put your finger on it. What word rhymes with** *flash? puddles...jump...splash.* **Circle the picture that shows the word that rhymes with** *flash.*

3. **Move down to the next row. Find the triangle. Put your finger on it. In the poem, the word** *day* **rhymes with** *play.* **What is another word that rhymes with** *play? rake...hay... cup.* **Circle the picture that shows another word that rhymes with** *play.*

WRITING

Students should draw a picture of something they like to do when it rains. For example, students could draw a picture of themselves holding an umbrella and standing in the rain. Then, students should write or tell a complete sentence about what they like to do when it rains. Record each student's answer under their picture.

Progress Check-Ups

HIGH-FREQUENCY WORDS

Turn to page 70. Use the following directions to administer the assessment. Directions in bold are to be read aloud. Students are to respond by circling the answer to each question.

Move through the assessment quickly to make sure you are assessing the student's ability to recognize the high-frequency words.

Look at the first page. I will say a word in each row, and you will circle the word I am saying.

1. **Find the square at the top of the page. Put your finger on the square. Now look at the three words in that row. Draw a circle around the word *so...so*.**

2. **Move down to the next row. Find the circle. Put your finger on it. Now look at the three words in that row. Draw a circle around the word *out...out*.**

3. **Move down to the next row. Find the triangle. Put your finger on it. Now look at the three words in that row. Draw a circle around the word *then...then*.**

PHONICS

Turn to page 71. Move through this assessment more slowly than you did for high-frequency words. Students will need more time to answer these questions.

Turn to the second page. I will tell you the sound a letter makes, and you will circle the picture that has the same sound.

1. **Find the square at the top of the page. Put your finger on it. Now look at the three pictures in that row: *glass...kite...hill*. The letter *s* makes the sound /s/. Draw a circle around the picture that has the sound of the letter *s*: *glass...kite...hill*.**

2. **Move down to the next row where you see the circle. Put your finger on it. Now look at the three pictures in that row: *bear...sack...toy*. The letter *k* makes the sound /k/. Draw a circle around the picture that has the sound of the letter *k*: *bear...sack...toy*.**

3. **Move down to the next row where you see the triangle. Put your finger on it. Now look at the three pictures in that row: *spoon...pencil...wagon*. The letter *w* makes the sound /w/. Draw a circle around the picture that has the sound of the letter *w*: *spoon...pencil...wagon*.**

4. **Move down to the next row where you see the heart. Put your finger on it. Now look at the three pictures in that row: *frog...moon...jar*. The letter *m* makes the sound /m/. Draw a circle around the picture that has the sound of the letter *m*: *frog...moon...jar*.**

LISTENING COMPREHENSION

Turn to page 72. You will read two selections and comprehension questions to students.

Turn to the last page of your assessment. Now I will read two selections. Then I will ask you some questions. Listen carefully. Here is the first selection.

Winter Clothing

Winter can be a lot of fun. It can be cold in winter. You may need to dress warmly to spend time outside.

You should wear a winter coat. Winter coats are big. They keep you warm. You also should wear mittens. Mittens go on your hands. They keep your fingers warm.

You need to wear a hat on your head when it is cold. Your hat should cover your ears. You should also wear warm boots. They keep your feet from getting too cold.

Here is the second selection.

Summer Clothing

In summer, it is warm outside. You need to make sure you do not get too hot in the summer.

You can wear shorts. They help your legs stay cool. You can also wear T-shirts. They keep you from getting too hot.

You can wear sandals. They will keep your feet cool. You might want to go swimming in the summer. You need to wear a swimsuit to go swimming.

Now I will ask you some questions. For each question, there are three pictures in a row. Draw a circle around the picture that shows the best answer. Listen carefully.

1. **Find the square at the top of the page and put your finger on it. Now look at the three pictures in that row. What do both selections tell about?** *winter...swimming... clothes.* **Circle the picture that shows what both selections tell about.**

2. **Move down to the next row. Find the circle. Put your finger on it. What do you wear to stay warm in the winter?** *sandals...shorts...boots.* **Circle the picture that shows what you would wear in the winter to stay warm.**

3. **Move down to the next row. Find the triangle. Put your finger on it. What is one difference between the two selections?** *only one tells about autumn...only one tells about winter... only one tells about spring.* **Circle the picture that shows a difference between the selections.**

WRITING

Students should draw a picture of something they wear in the summer. Then, students should write or tell a complete sentence about what they do when they are wearing it. Record each student's answer under their picture.

Teacher Scripting: Unit 5 Week 5 Progress Check-Up

HIGH-FREQUENCY WORDS

Turn to page 73. Use the following directions to administer the assessment. Directions in bold are to be read aloud. Students are to respond by circling the answer to each question.

Move through the assessment quickly to make sure you are assessing the student's ability to recognize the high-frequency words.

Look at the first page. I will say a word in each row, and you will circle the word I am saying.

1. **Find the square at the top of the page. Put your finger on the square. Now look at the three words in that row. Draw a circle around the word *new...new*.**

2. **Move down to the next row. Find the circle. Put your finger on it. Now look at the three words in that row. Draw a circle around the word *too...too*.**

3. **Move down to the next row. Find the triangle. Put your finger on it. Now look at the three words in that row. Draw a circle around the word *when...when*.**

PHONICS

Turn to page 74. Move through this assessment more slowly than you did for the high-frequency words. Students will need more time to answer these questions.

Turn to the second page. I will tell you the sound a letter makes, and you will circle the picture that has the same sound.

1. **Find the square at the top of the page. Put your finger on it. Now look at the three pictures in that row: *barn...leaf...desk*. The letter *l* makes the sound /l/. Draw a circle around the picture that has the sound of the letter *l*: *barn...leaf...desk*.**

2. **Move down to the next row where you see the circle. Put your finger on it. Now look at the three pictures in that row: *rake...duck...nest*. The letter *r* makes the sound /r/. Draw a circle around the picture that has the sound of the letter *r*: *rake...duck...nest*.**

3. **Move down to the next row where you see the triangle. Put your finger on it. Now look at the three pictures in that row: *corn...eight...door*. The letter *n* makes the sound /n/. Draw a circle around the picture that has the end sound of the letter *n*: *corn...eight...door*.**

4. **Move down to the next row where you see the heart. Put your finger on it. Now look at the three pictures in that row: *crow...zero...tiger*. The letter *z* makes the sound /z/. Draw a circle around the picture that has the sound of the letter *z*: *crow...zero...tiger*.**

LISTENING COMPREHENSION

Turn to page 75. You will read a selection and comprehension questions to students.

Turn to the last page of your assessment. Now I will read a selection. Then I will ask you some questions. Listen carefully.

If It Snows

MOLLY: Did you hear it might snow tomorrow?

SAM: Yes. I love snow!

MOLLY: What will you do if it snows?

SAM: I might go sledding.

MOLLY: That sounds like fun.

SAM: What will you do?

MOLLY: I might build a snowman.

SAM: I like building snowmen.

MOLLY: Mrs. Li, what will you do if it snows tomorrow?

MRS. LI: I will go outside. I will have to clean snow off my car.

SAM: That does not sound like too much fun.

MRS. LI: Maybe not. I will take my son outside to play in the snow too. That will be fun.

Now I am going to ask you some questions about the selection. For each question, there are three pictures in a row. Draw a circle around the picture that shows the best answer. Listen carefully.

1. **Find the square at the top of the page and put your finger on it. Now look at the three pictures in that row. What does Molly say she might do if it snows?** *sled... sleep...build a snowman.* **Circle the picture that shows what Molly says she will do if it snows.**

2. **Move down to the next row. Find the circle. Put your finger on it. How does Sam feel about the snow?** *unhappy...excited...bored.* **Circle the picture that shows how Sam feels about the snow.**

3. **Move down to the next row. Find the triangle. Put your finger on it. Which character will clean off a car if it snows?** *Mrs. Li...Sam...Molly.* **Circle the picture that shows who will clean off a car if it snows.**

WRITING

Students should draw a picture of what they might do if it snowed. For example, students might draw a picture of kids sledding. Then, students should write or tell a complete sentence about what they might do if it snowed. Record each student's answer under their picture.

Progress Check-Ups

Answer Key

UNIT 1, WEEK 1 ANSWER KEY

Name___________ Mission Accomplished

High-Frequency Words

■	do	(I)	go
●	(the)	for	two
▲	she	for	(am)

Unit 1 Week 1 Progress Check-Up **1**

Mission Accomplished Name___________

Phonics

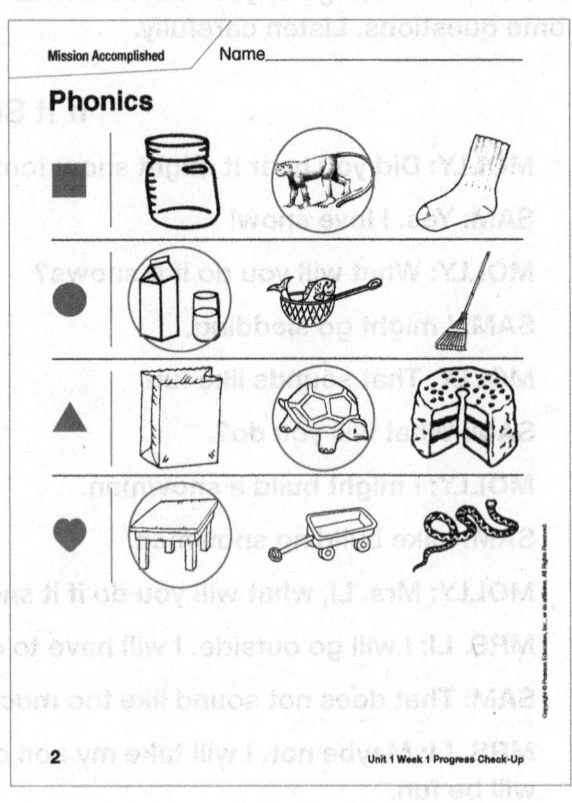

Unit 1 Week 1 Progress Check-Up **2**

Name___________ Mission Accomplished

Listening Comprehension

Writing – Draw and Tell

Draw a picture that shows something you would like to do. Then write or tell something about your drawing.

Unit 1 Week 1 Progress Check-Up **3**

  Progress Check-Ups

UNIT 1, WEEK 2 ANSWER KEY

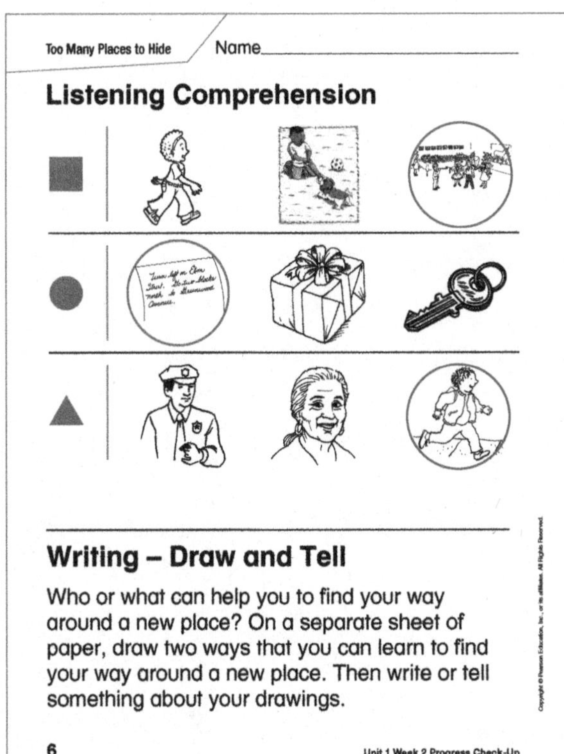

Writing – Draw and Tell

Who or what can help you to find your way around a new place? On a separate sheet of paper, draw two ways that you can learn to find your way around a new place. Then write or tell something about your drawings.

UNIT 1, WEEK 3 ANSWER KEY

UNIT 1, WEEK 2 ANSWER KEY

High-Frequency Words

At the Library

Name

■ for (have) go

● (he) it two

▲ she for (is)

Phonics

At the Library Name

Listening Comprehension

Name At the Library

Writing – Draw and Tell

Think of a real place that you like to go to. On a separate sheet of paper, draw a picture of the place or of something you see there. Then write or tell something about what you have drawn.

UNIT 1, WEEK 4 ANSWER KEY

High-Frequency Words

■   to   the   (we)

●   (my)   and   for

▲   can   of   make

10   Unit 1 Week 4 Progress Check-Up

Phonics

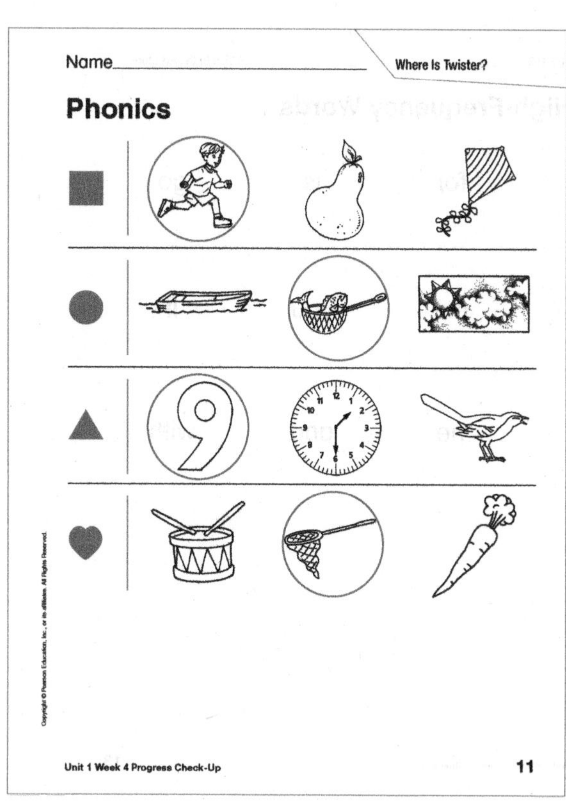

Unit 1 Week 4 Progress Check-Up   11

Listening Comprehension

Writing – Draw and Tell

On a separate sheet of paper, draw something you might see at a planetarium. Then write or tell something about your drawing.

12   Unit 1 Week 4 Progress Check-Up

Progress Check-Ups   **T73**

Name _____________________ A Visit to the Art Store

High-Frequency Words

■ (for) is go

● (me) you it

▲ he and (with)

Unit 1 Week 5 Progress Check-Up 13

A Visit to the Art Store Name _____________________

Phonics

14 Unit 1 Week 5 Progress Check-Up

Name _____________________ A Visit to the Art Store

Listening Comprehension

Writing – Draw and Tell

On a separate sheet of paper, draw a picture of
something you might see at a farmers market.
Then write or tell something about your drawing.

Unit 1 Week 5 Progress Check-Up 15

UNIT 2, WEEK 1 ANSWER KEY

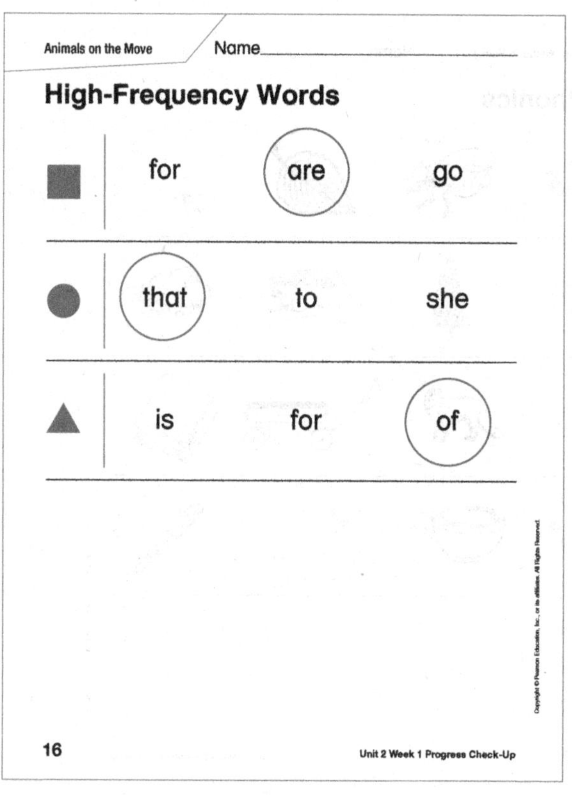

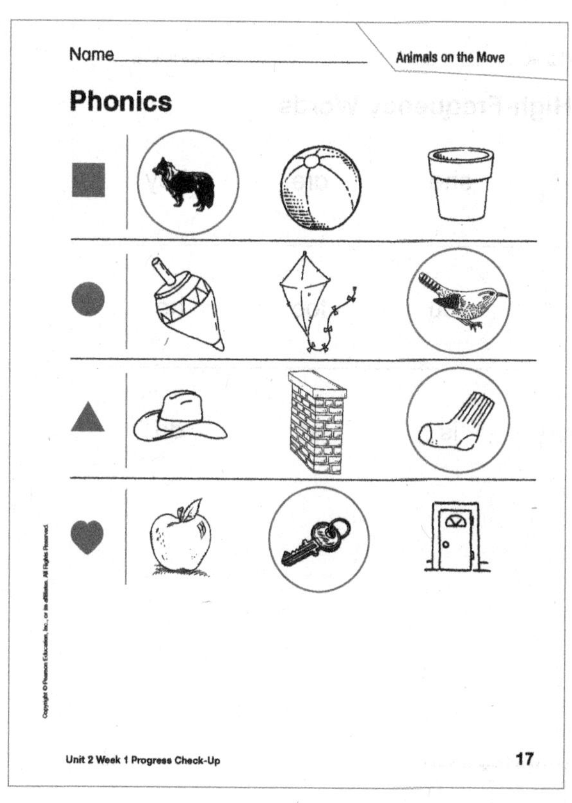

Progress Check-Ups

UNIT 2, WEEK 2 ANSWER KEY

UNIT 2, WEEK 3 ANSWER KEY

High-Frequency Words

are   four   too

five   she   it

here   for   is

Phonics

Listening Comprehension

Writing – Informational

On a separate sheet of paper, draw a picture of an animal. Then write or tell one food you think the animal eats.

UNIT 2, WEEK 5 ANSWER KEY

High-Frequency Words

Run, Jump, and Swim — Name

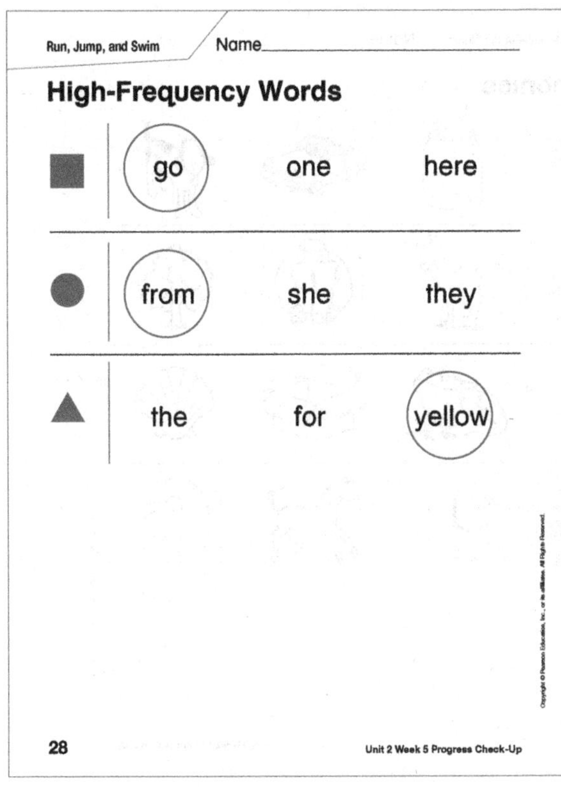

Phonics

Name — Run, Jump, and Swim

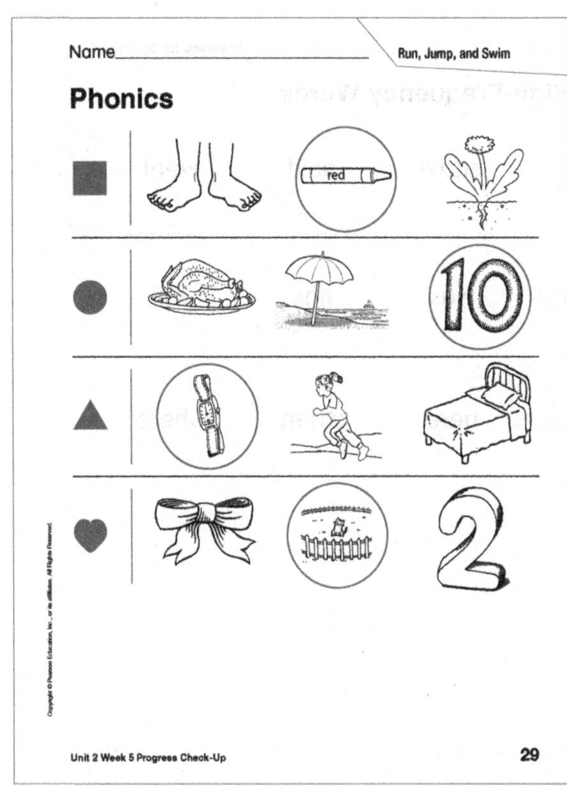

Unit 2 Week 5 Progress Check-Up

Unit 2 Week 5 Progress Check-Up

Listening Comprehension

Run, Jump, and Swim — Name

Writing – Informational

On a separate sheet of paper, draw a picture of your favorite way to play. Then tell or write about three different ways you like to play.

Unit 2 Week 5 Progress Check-Up

Progress Check-Ups

Name________________ How Anansi Got His Stories

High-Frequency Words

■   show   (said)   went

●   (was)   has   will

▲   here   when   (where)

How Anansi Got His Stories   Name________________

Phonics

Name________________ How Anansi Got His Stories

Listening Comprehension

Writing – Fiction

Think of a fiction story you would like to write. Draw a picture of the characters and setting of your fiction story. The tell or write a sentence telling about an event in the story.

UNIT 3, WEEK 2 ANSWER KEY

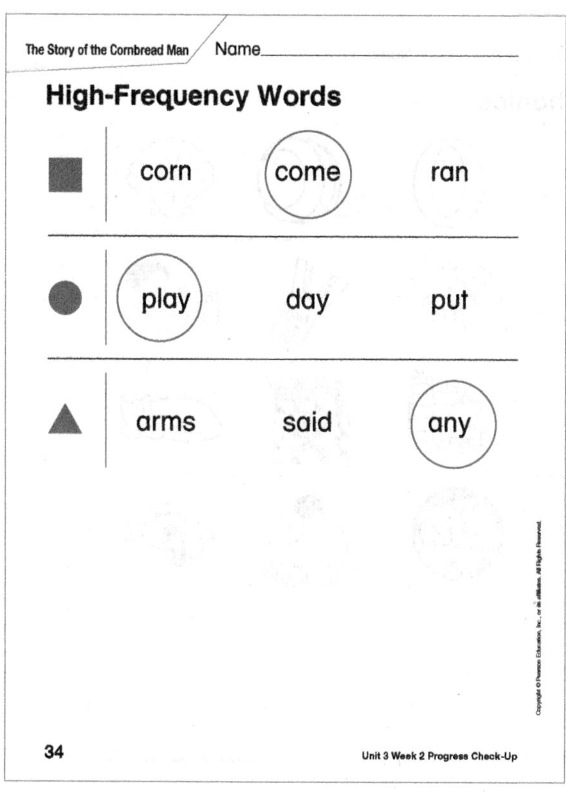

UNIT 3, WEEK 3 ANSWER KEY

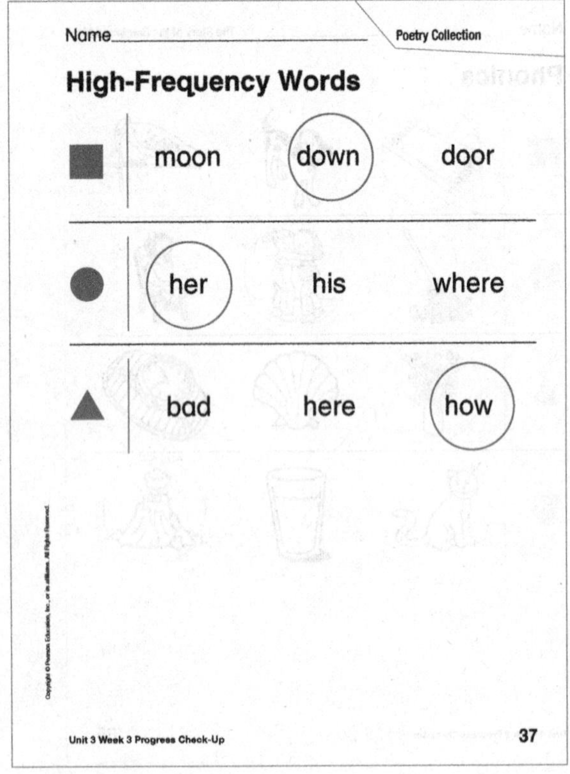

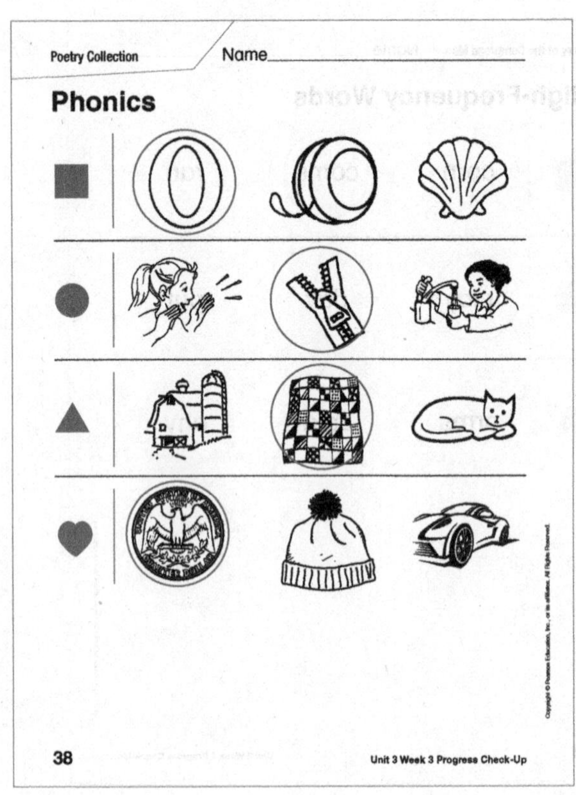

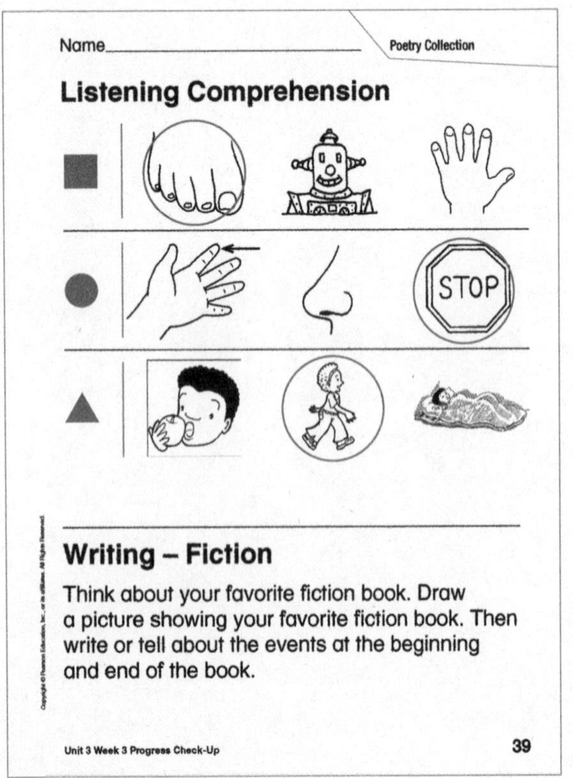

Progress Check-Ups

UNIT 3, WEEK 4 ANSWER KEY

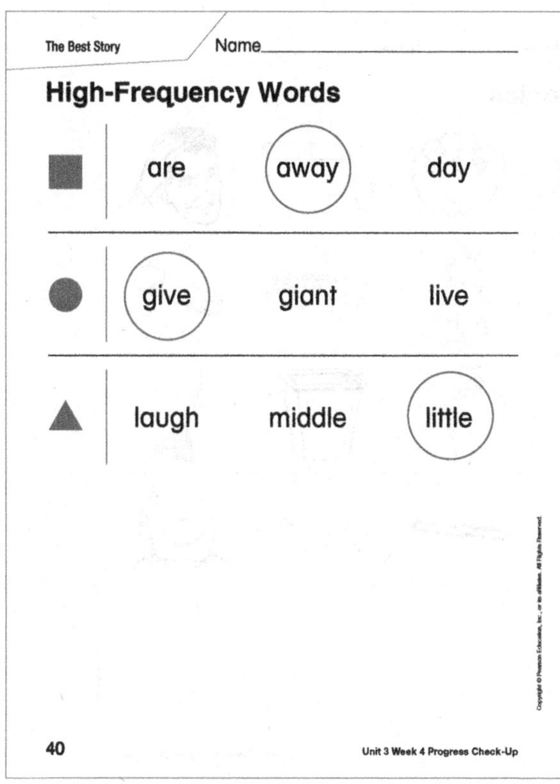

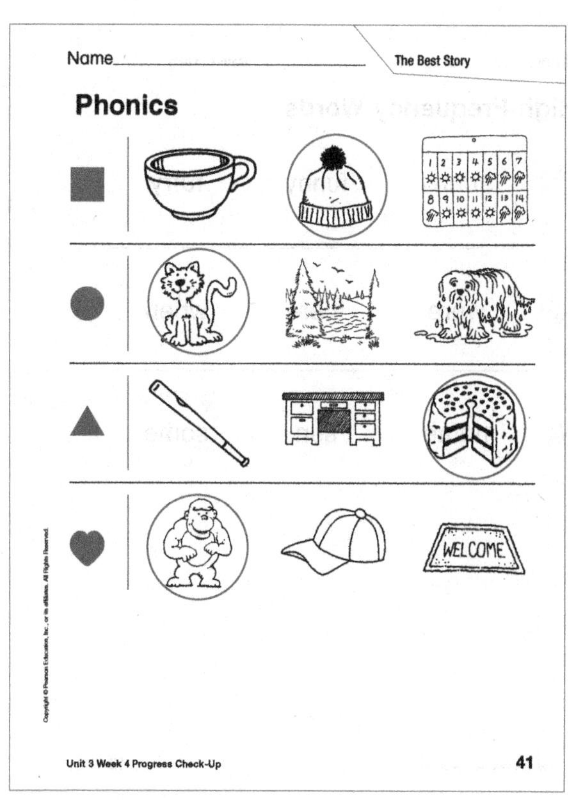

Writing – Fiction

Draw a picture of a make-believe person you would like to tell a story about. Then write or tell one thing the person in your story would do.

High-Frequency Words

■ sunny | (funny) | furry

● (were) | there | when

▲ home | sun | (some)

Phonics

44

Listening Comprehension

Writing – Fiction

Draw a picture of Pegasus, the flying horse from the story. Then write or tell something Pegasus could do in a story.

UNIT 4, WEEK 1 ANSWER KEY

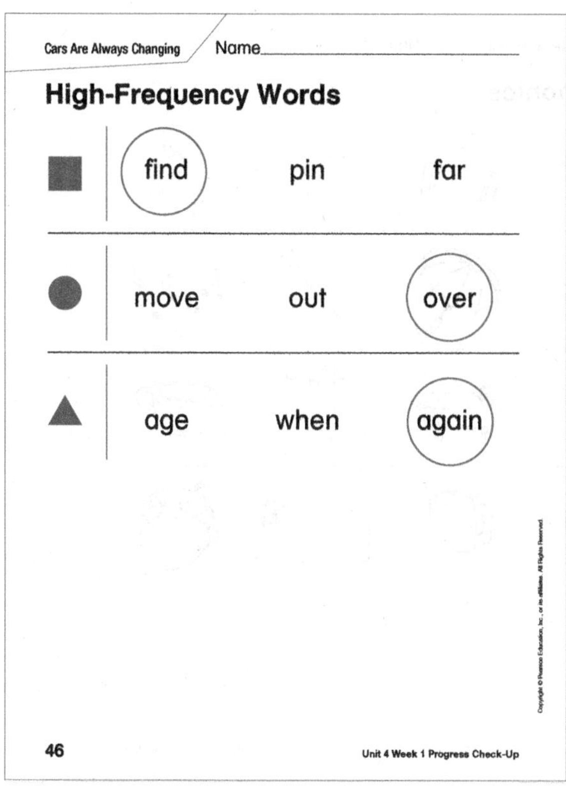

Progress Check-Ups

UNIT 4, WEEK 2 ANSWER KEY

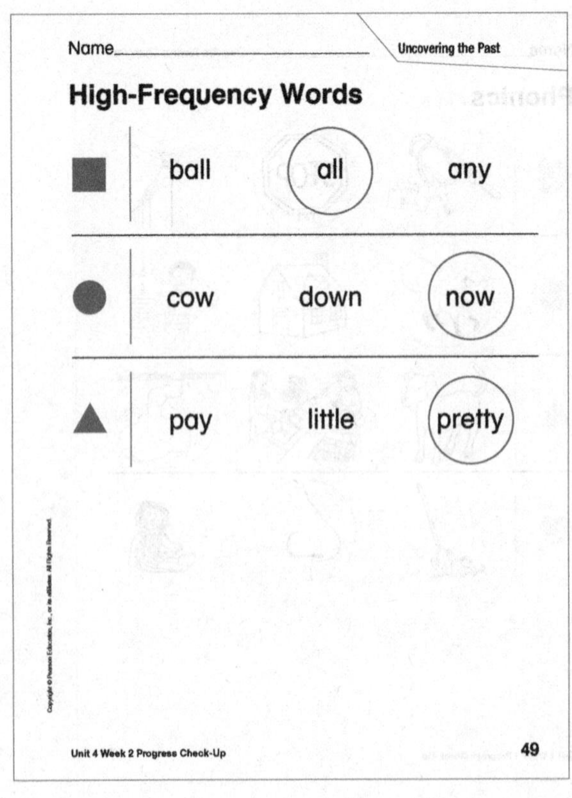

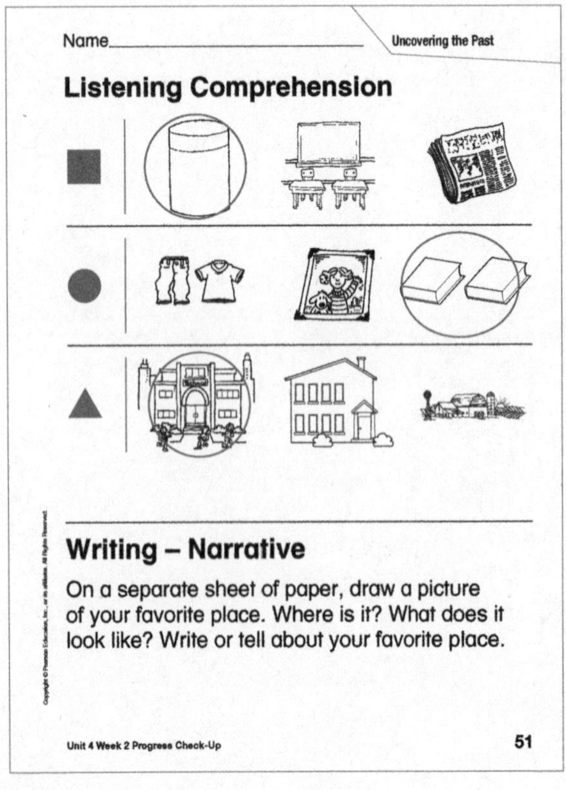

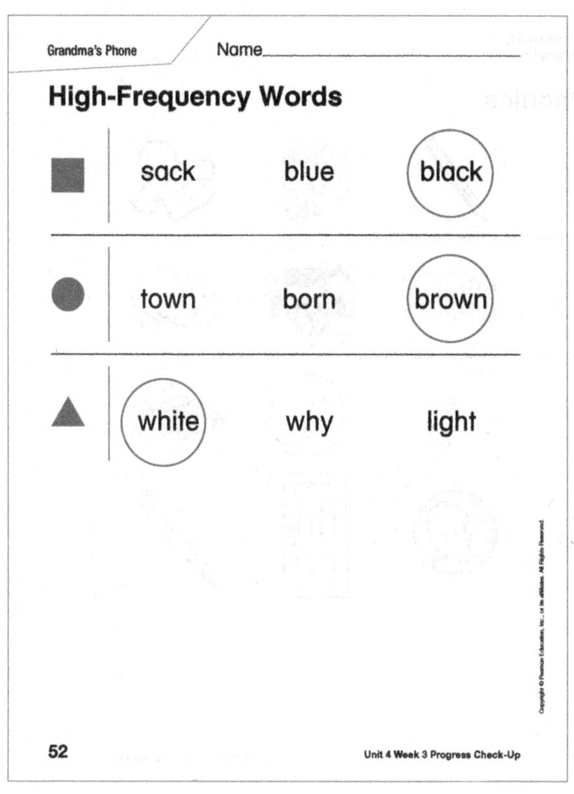

Grandma's Phone
Name
High-Frequency Words
sack   blue   black
town   born   brown
white   why   light
52
Unit 4 Week 3 Progress Check-Up

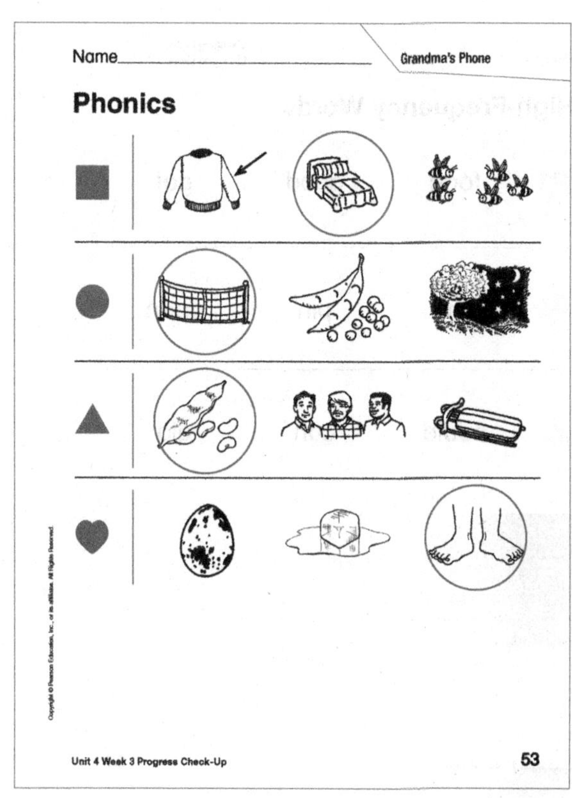

Name
Grandma's Phone
Phonics
Unit 4 Week 3 Progress Check-Up
53

Grandma's Phone
Name
Listening Comprehension
Writing – Narrative
On a separate sheet of paper, draw a picture of a
problem you had to solve. How did you solve the
problem? Write or tell about the steps you took to
solve the problem.
54
Unit 4 Week 3 Progress Check-Up

UNIT 4, WEEK 4 ANSWER KEY

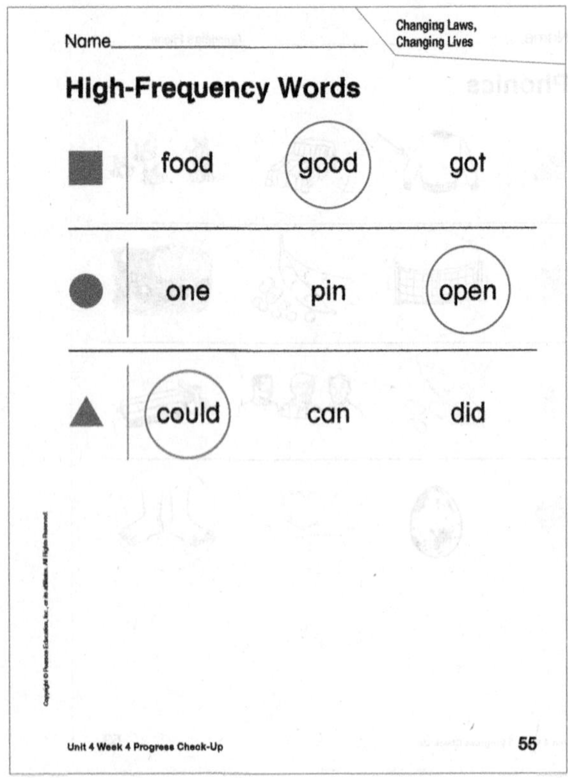

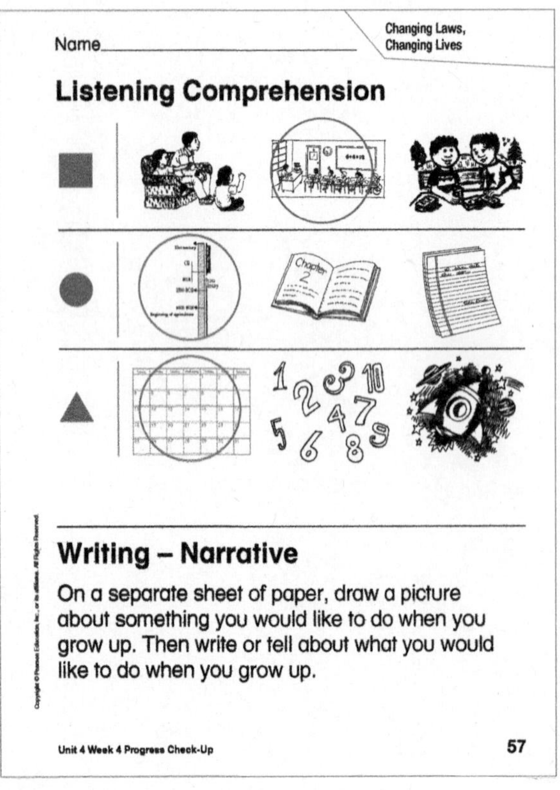

Progress Check-Ups

UNIT 4, WEEK 5 ANSWER KEY

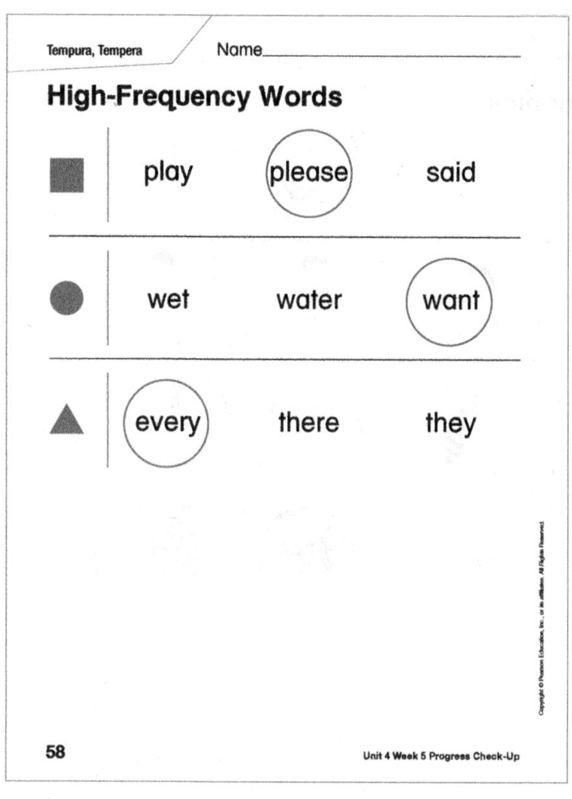

Writing – Narrative

On a separate sheet of paper, draw a picture of a tradition that you have with your family. Write or tell two sentences about the tradition. Check to make sure the first letters of names have capital letters.

Progress Check-Ups

UNIT 5, WEEK 1 ANSWER KEY

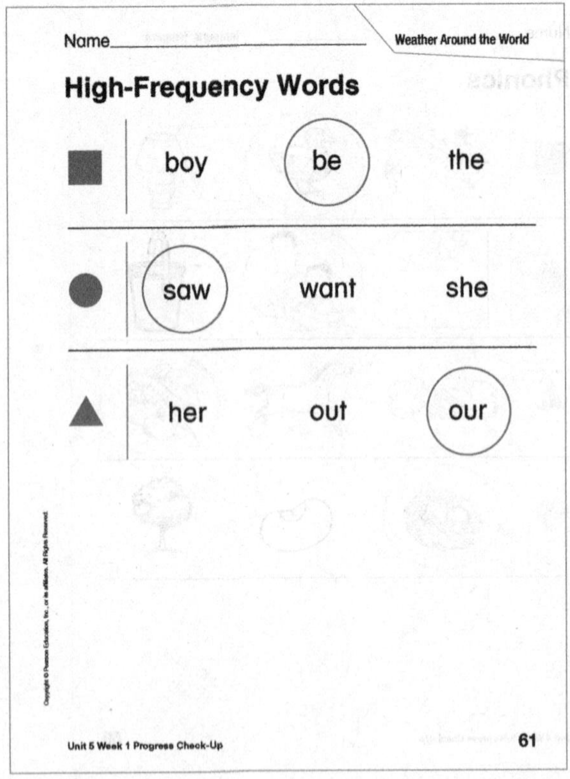

Writing – Literary Nonfiction

You know that snow is a weather event. On a separate sheet of paper, draw a picture of a different weather event. Then write or tell a question and an answer about that weather event.

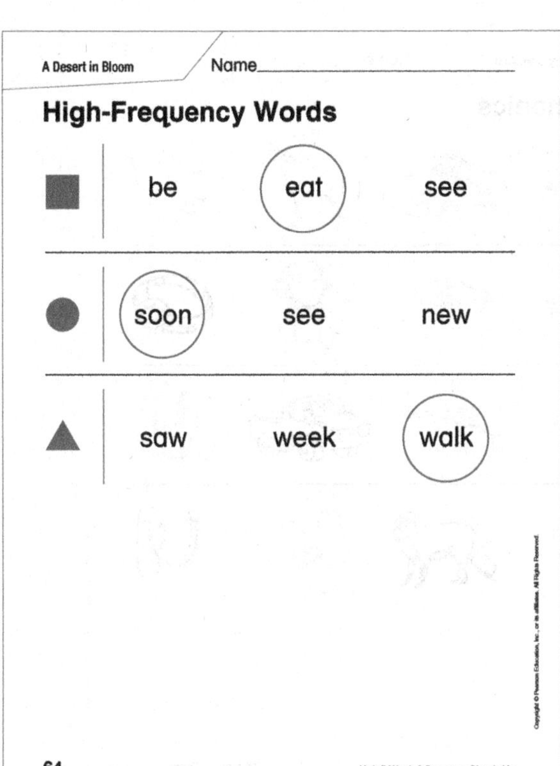

A Desert in Bloom — Name____________

High-Frequency Words

■	be	(eat)	see
●	(soon)	see	new
▲	saw	week	(walk)

64 — Unit 5 Week 2 Progress Check-Up

Name____________ — **A Desert in Bloom**

Phonics

Unit 5 Week 2 Progress Check-Up — 65

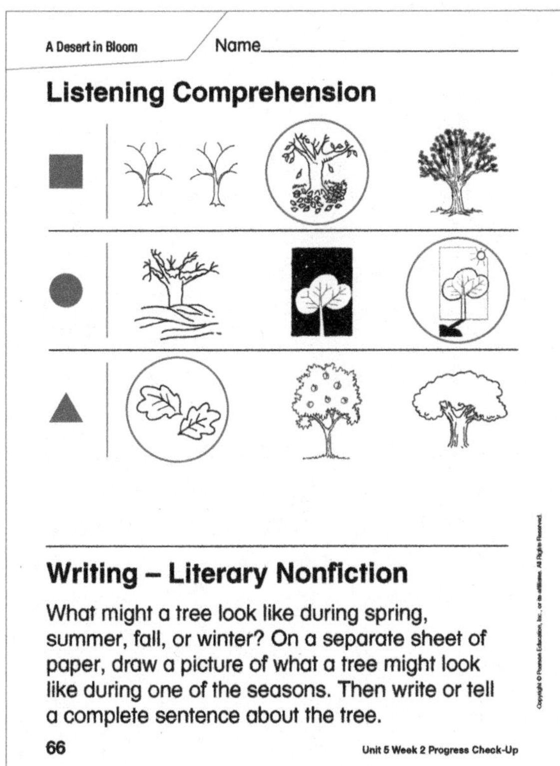

A Desert in Bloom — Name____________

Listening Comprehension

Writing – Literary Nonfiction

What might a tree look like during spring, summer, fall, or winter? On a separate sheet of paper, draw a picture of what a tree might look like during one of the seasons. Then write or tell a complete sentence about the tree.

66 — Unit 5 Week 2 Progress Check-Up

Name_______________________ Poetry Collection

High-Frequency Words

■ (who)   soon   why

● (into)   do   one

▲ they   were   (there)

Unit 5 Week 3 Progress Check-Up   67

Poetry Collection   Name_______________________

Phonics

68   Unit 5 Week 3 Progress Check-Up

Name_______________________ Poetry Collection

Listening Comprehension

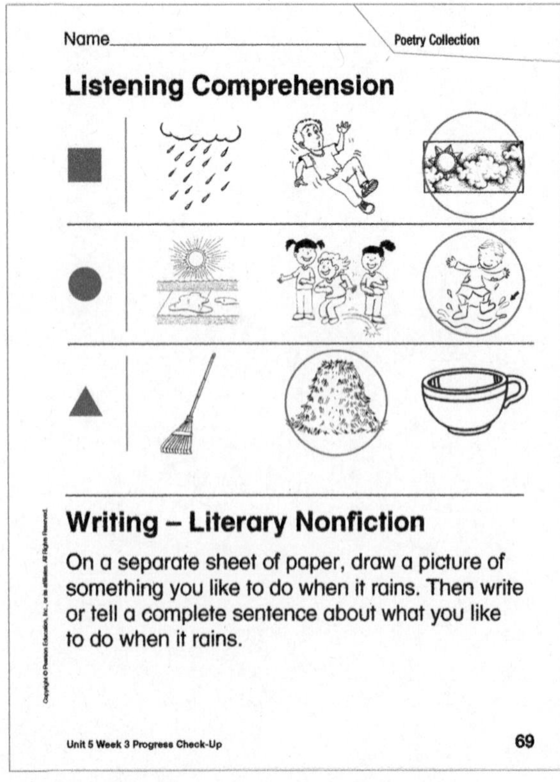

Writing – Literary Nonfiction

On a separate sheet of paper, draw a picture of
something you like to do when it rains. Then write
or tell a complete sentence about what you like
to do when it rains.

Unit 5 Week 3 Progress Check-Up   69

Progress Check-Ups

UNIT 5, WEEK 4 ANSWER KEY

UNIT 5, WEEK 5 ANSWER KEY

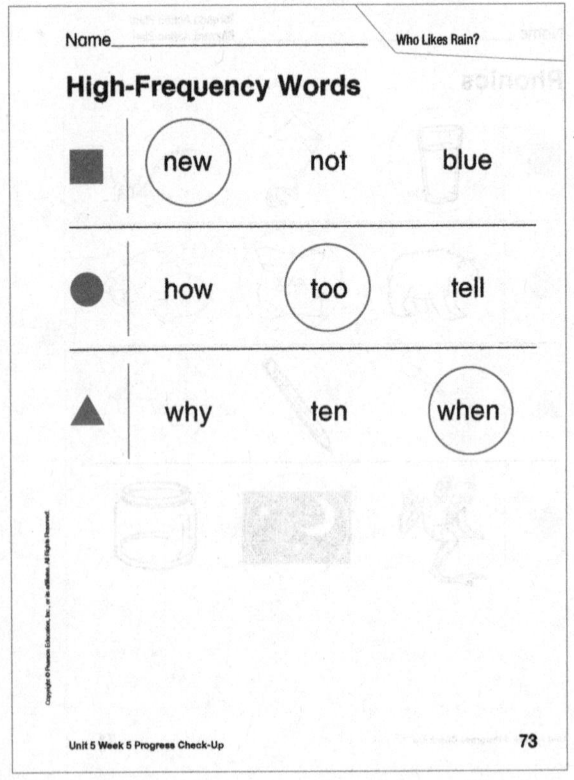

Name______________   Who Likes Rain?

High-Frequency Words

■ | (new) not blue

● | how (too) tell

▲ | why ten (when)

Unit 5 Week 5 Progress Check-Up **73**

Who Likes Rain? Name______________

Phonics

74 Unit 5 Week 5 Progress Check-Up

Name______________   Who Likes Rain?

Listening Comprehension

Writing – Literary Nonfiction

What might you do if it snowed? On a separate sheet of paper, draw a picture of what you might do if it snowed. Then write or tell a complete sentence telling what you might do if it snowed.

Unit 5 Week 5 Progress Check-Up **75**

Progress Check-Ups

High-Frequency Words

■	do	I	go
●	the	for	two
▲	she	for	am

Name________________

Phonics

   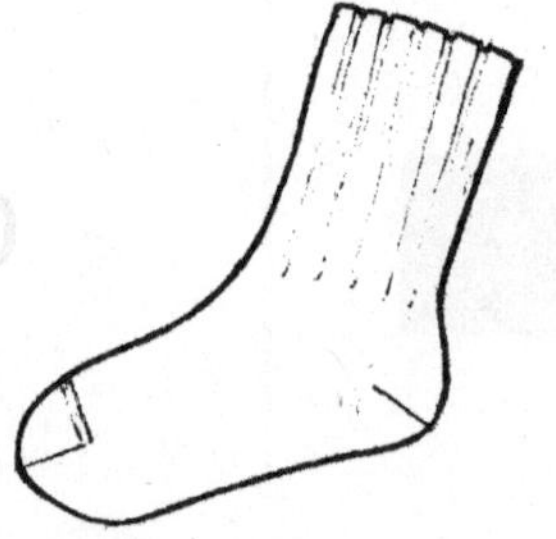

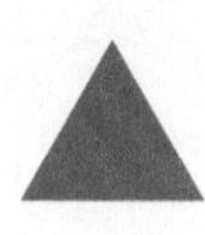   

 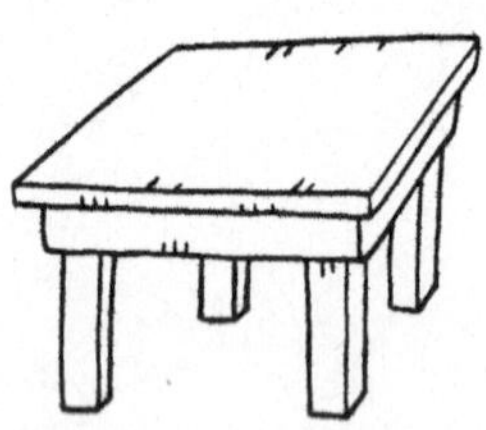  

2

Listening Comprehension

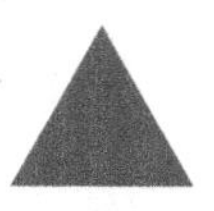   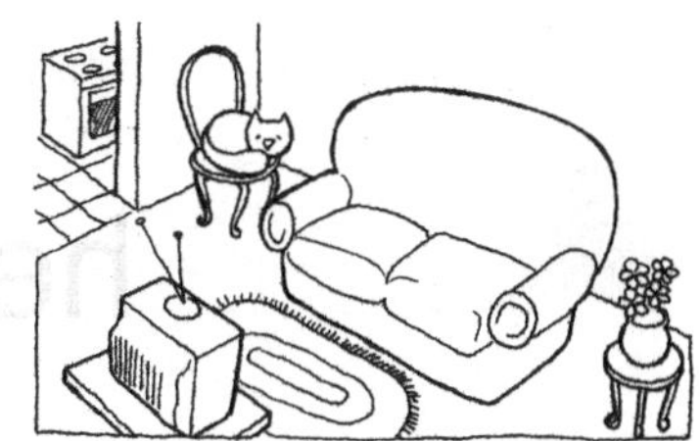

Writing – Draw and Tell

Draw a picture that shows something you would like to do. Then write or tell something about your drawing.

Name_______________________

High-Frequency Words

■	for	like	the
●	to	go	me
▲	he	do	a

Phonics

 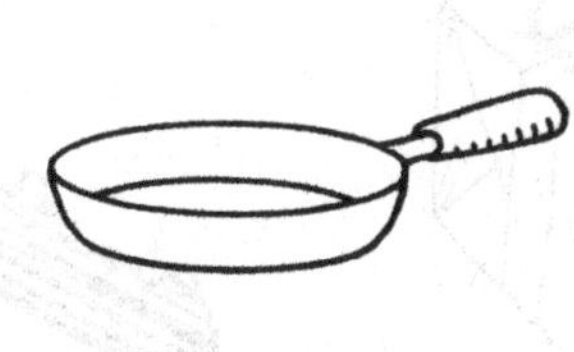  

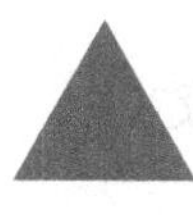 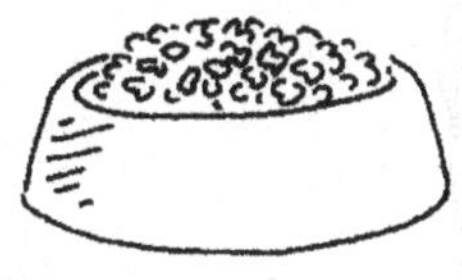  

   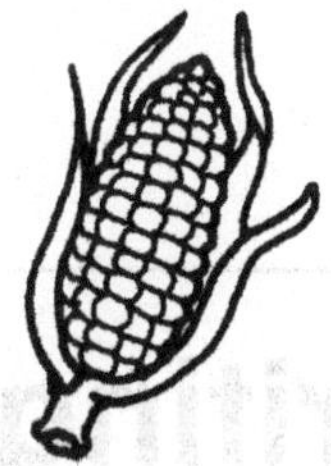

Name______________________

Listening Comprehension

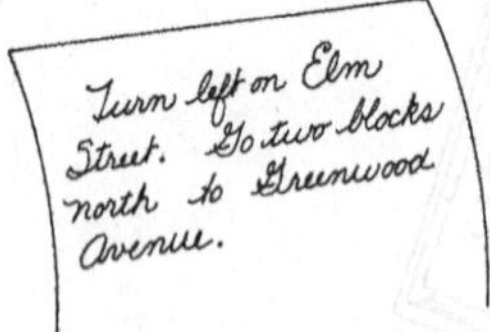

Writing – Draw and Tell

Who or what can help you to find your way around a new place? On a separate sheet of paper, draw two ways that you can learn to find your way around a new place. Then write or tell something about your drawings.

Unit 1 Week 2 Progress Check-Up

High-Frequency Words

 for   have   go

 he   it   two

▲ she   for   is

Name_______________________

Phonics

  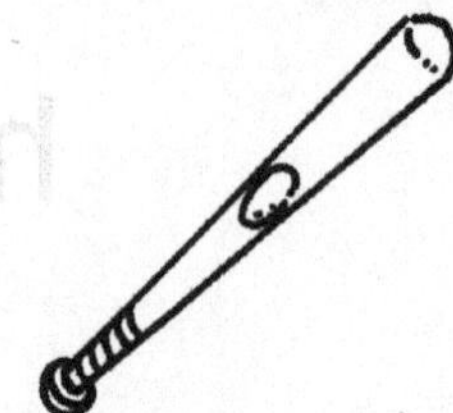 

  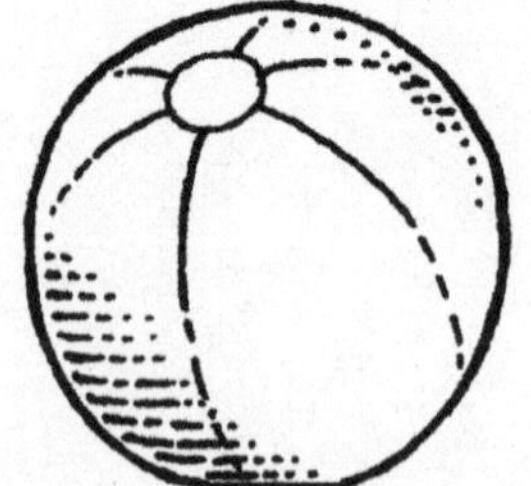 

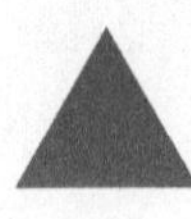  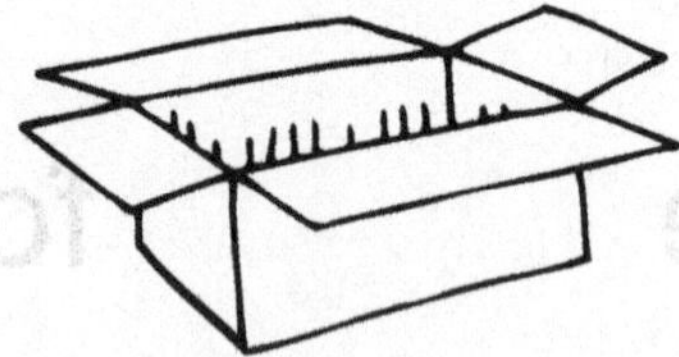 

   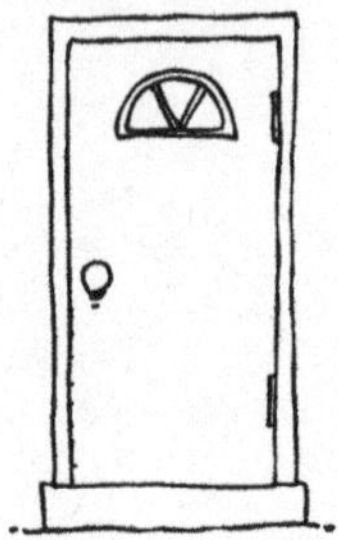

Unit 1 Week 3 Progress Check-Up

Listening Comprehension

  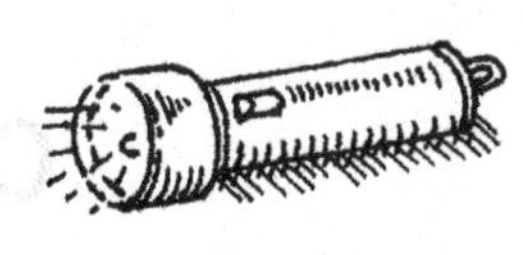 

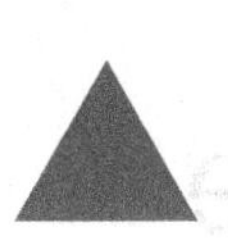   

Writing – Draw and Tell

Think of a real place that you like to go to. On a separate sheet of paper, draw a picture of the place or of something you see there. Then write or tell something about what you have drawn.

Name __________________

High-Frequency Words

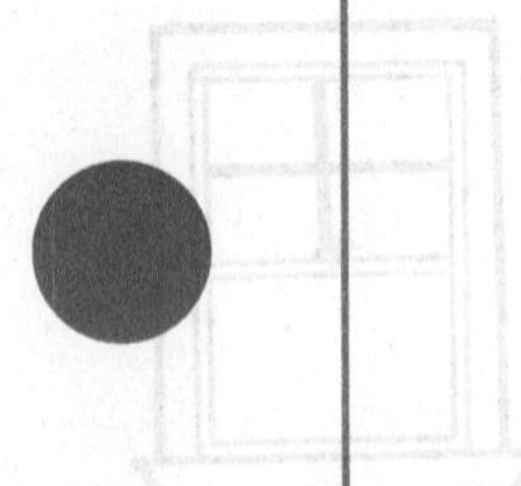

	to	the	we

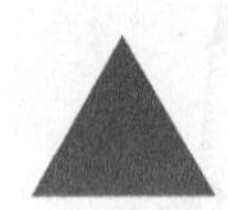

	my	and	for

	can	of	make

Phonics

 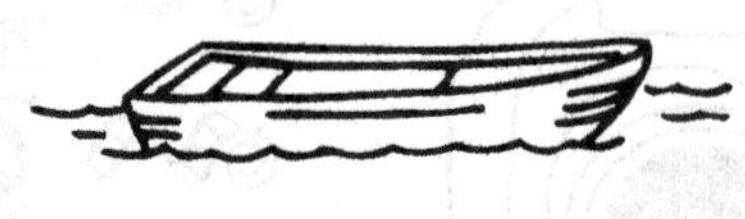  

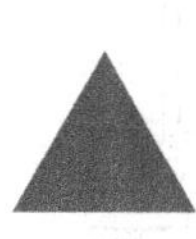   

  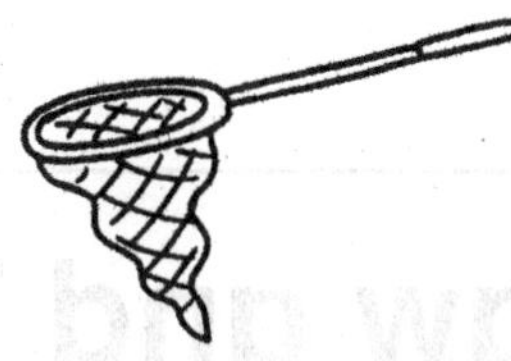 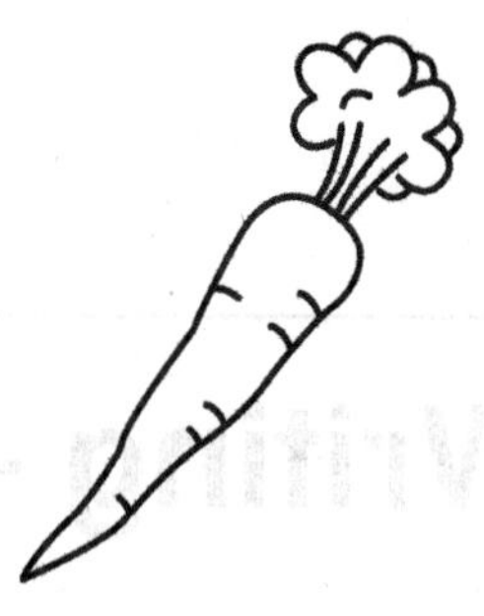

Name________________________

Listening Comprehension

 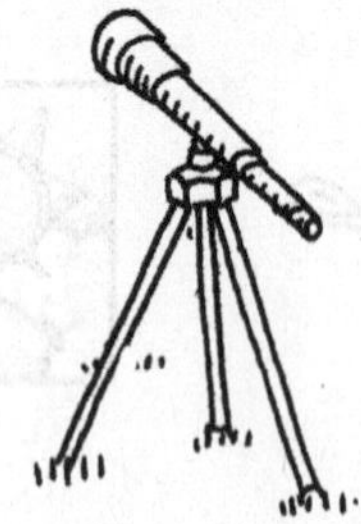  

Writing – Draw and Tell

On a separate sheet of paper, draw something you might see at a planetarium. Then write or tell something about your drawing.

High-Frequency Words

for   is   go

me   you   it

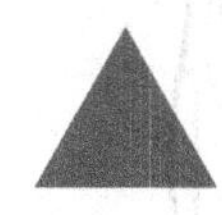

he   and   with

Name_______________________

Phonics

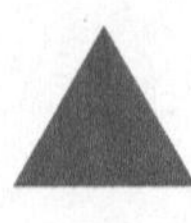  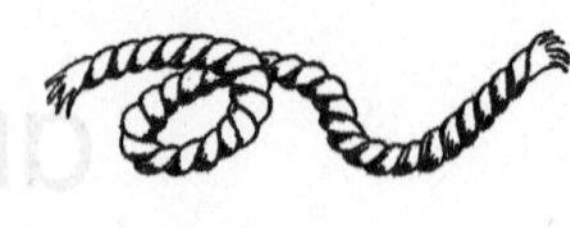 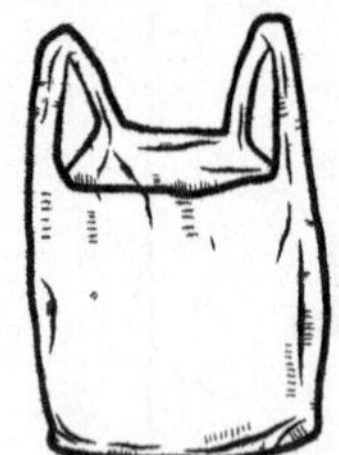

14

Name________________________

Listening Comprehension

Writing – Draw and Tell

On a separate sheet of paper, draw a picture of something you might see at a farmers market. Then write or tell something about your drawing.

High-Frequency Words

 for   are   go

 that   to   she

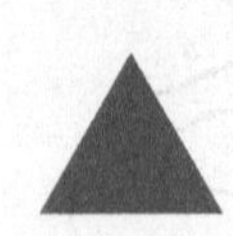 is   for   of

Phonics

  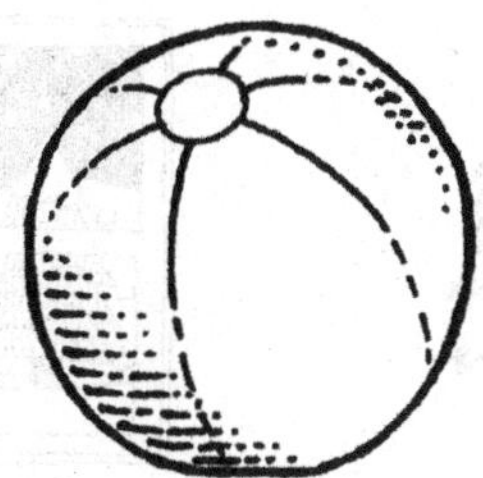 

 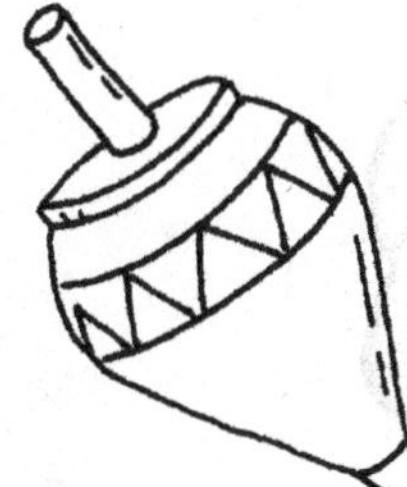 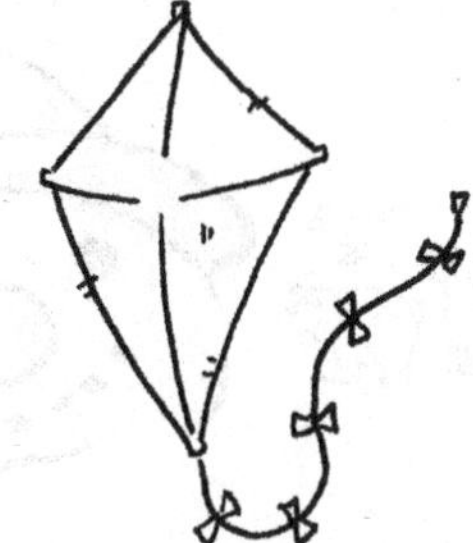 

  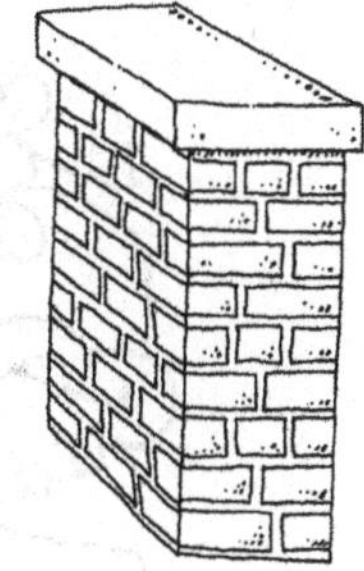 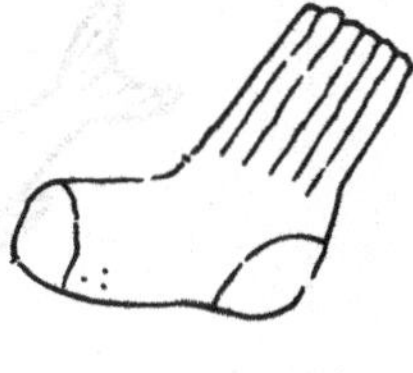

Name_______________________

Listening Comprehension

   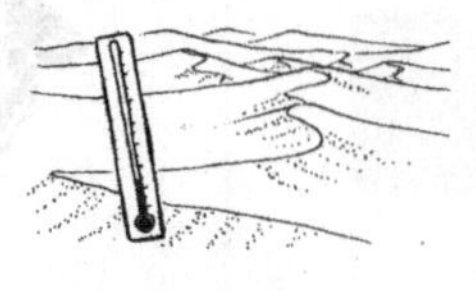

Writing – Informational

On a separate sheet of paper, draw a picture of an animal. Then write or tell one detail about the animal.

High-Frequency Words

■	she	are	they
●	you	too	he
▲	is	so	do

Phonics

Name_______________________________

Listening Comprehension

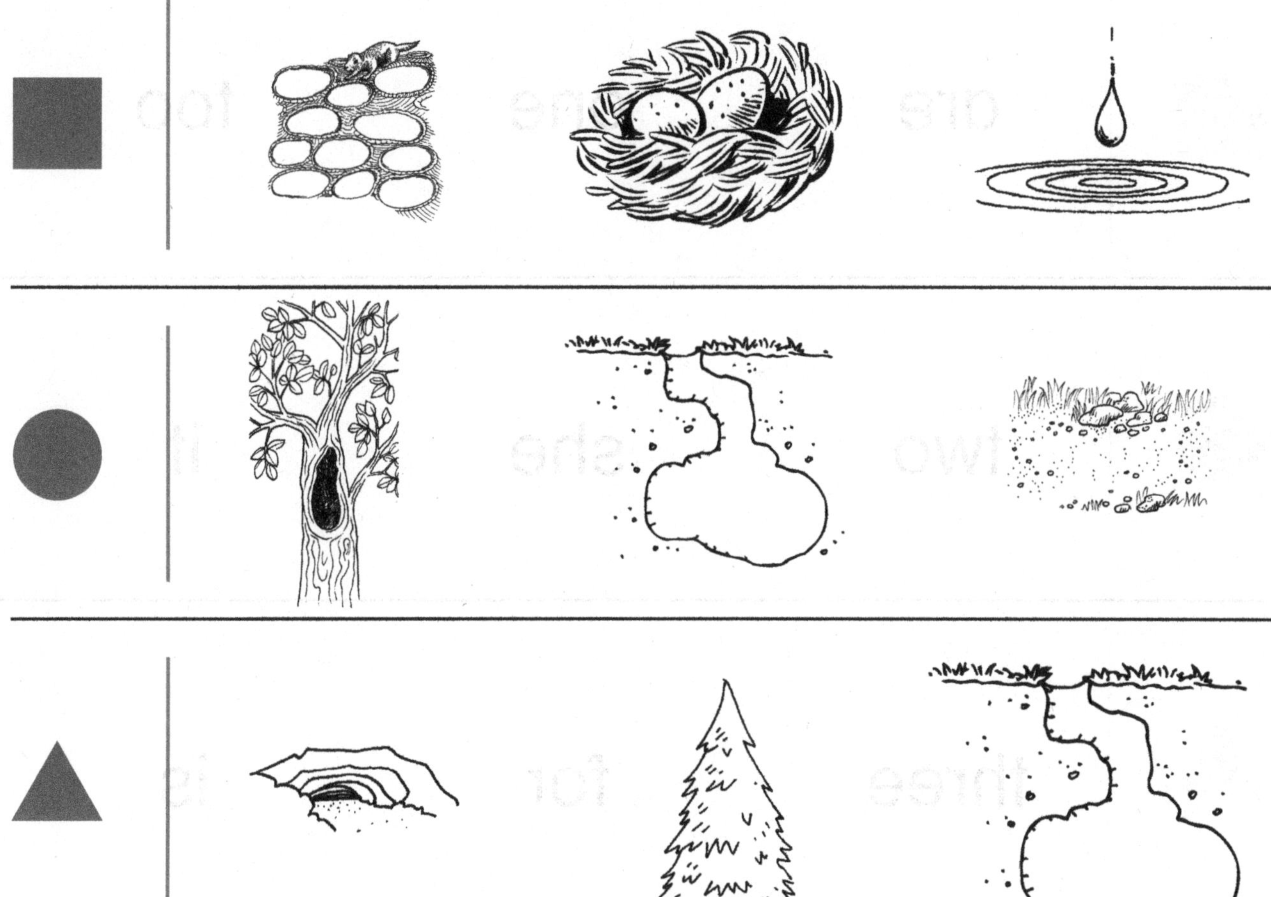

Writing – Informational

On a separate sheet of paper, draw a picture of an animal home. Then write or tell what kind of animal lives in the home.

High-Frequency Words

   are   one   too

   two   she   it

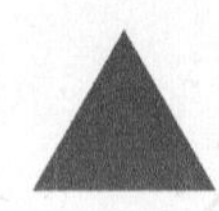   three   for   is

22

Phonics

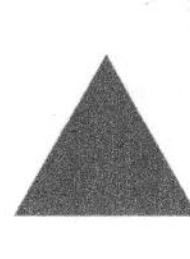 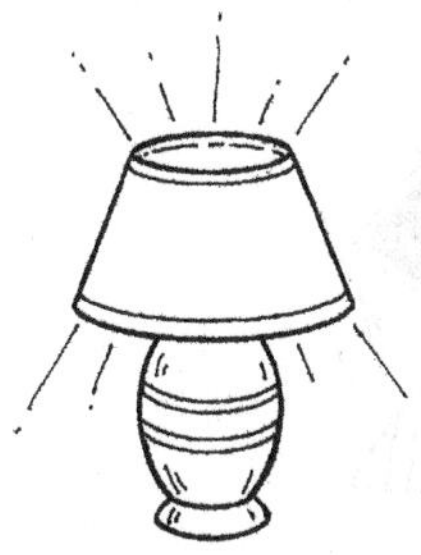  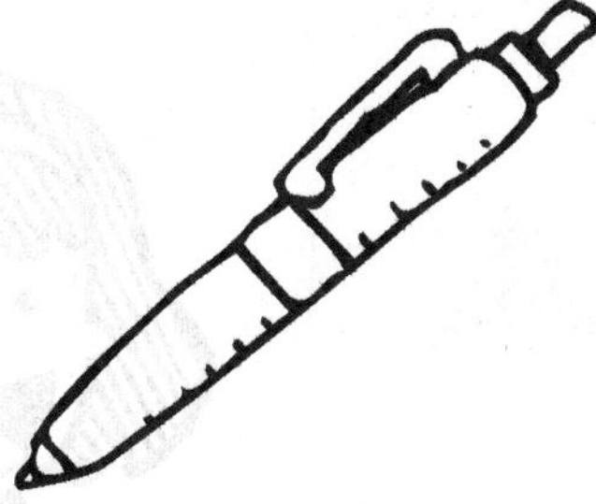

 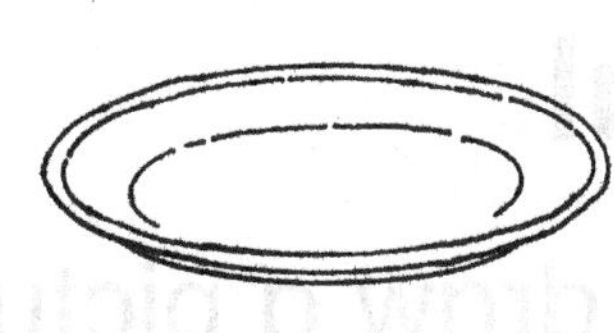  

Name

Listening Comprehension

 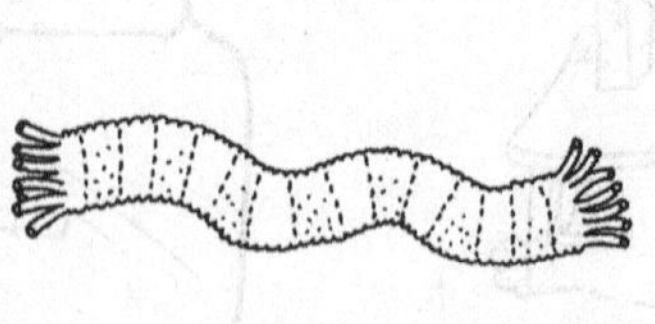  

Writing – Informational

On a separate sheet of paper, draw a picture of something you like to wear. Then write or tell one detail about the thing you like to wear.

Name_______________________

High-Frequency Words

are   four   too

five   she   it

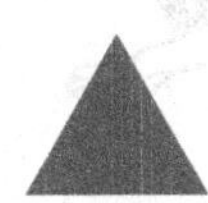

here   for   is

Name_______________________

Phonics

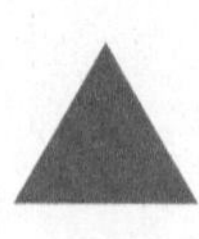   

26

Listening Comprehension

 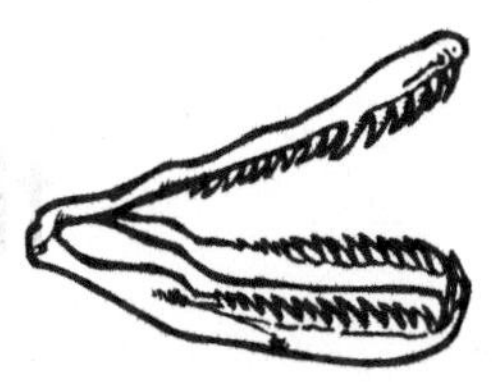  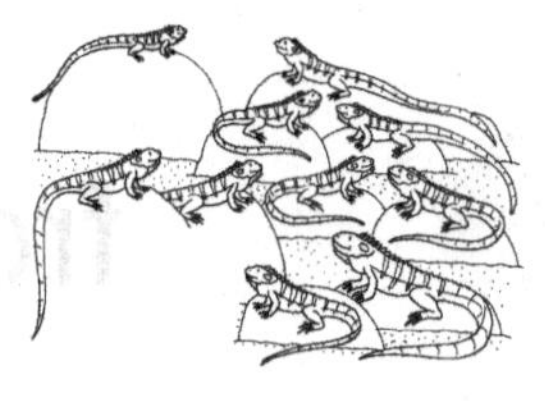

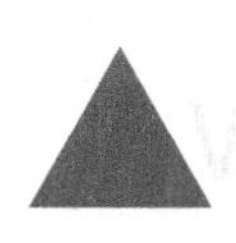   

Writing – Informational

On a separate sheet of paper, draw a picture of an animal. Then write or tell one food you think the animal eats.

Name________________________

High-Frequency Words

■	go	one	here
●	from	she	they
▲	the	for	yellow

Phonics

 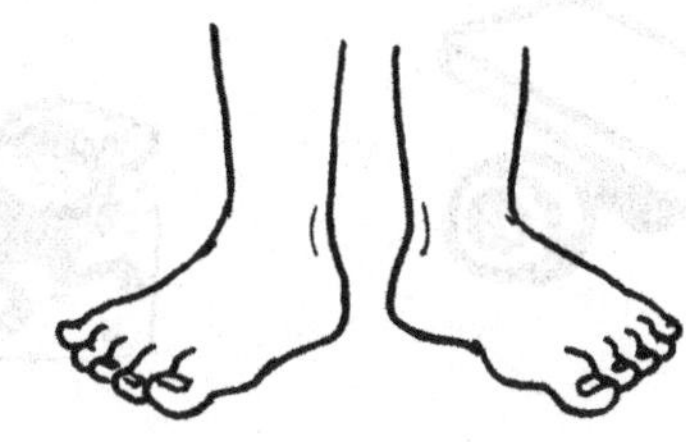  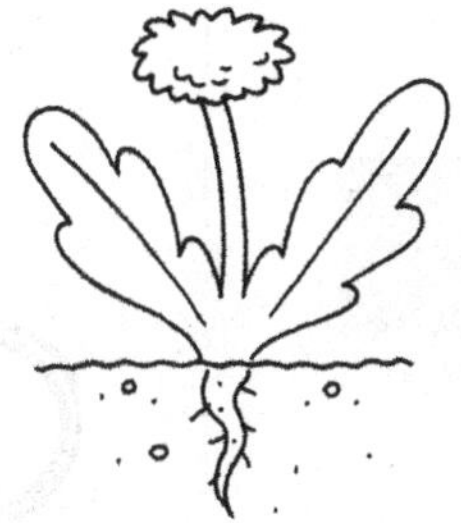

   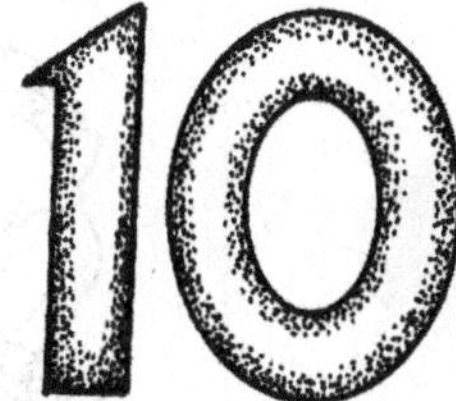

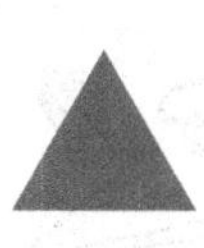   

 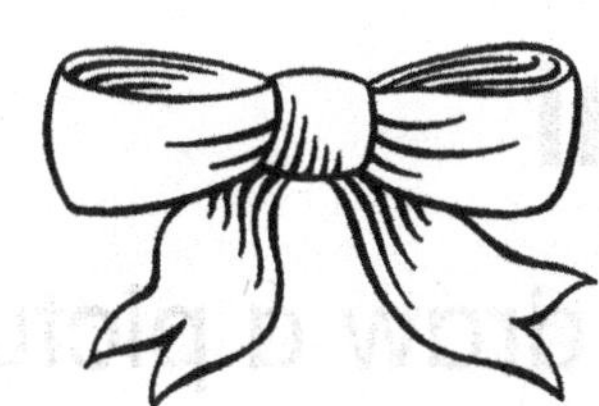  

Unit 2 Week 5 Progress Check-Up

Listening Comprehension

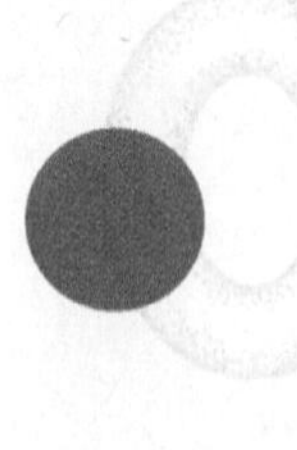   

   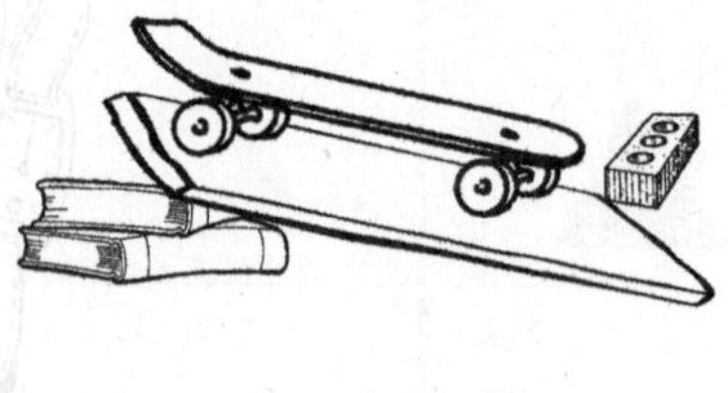

Writing – Informational

On a separate sheet of paper, draw a picture of your favorite way to play. Then tell or write about three different ways you like to play.

30

High-Frequency Words

   show   said   went

   was   has   will

   here   when   where

Name________________

Phonics

Unit 3 Week 1 Progress Check-Up

Name_______________________

Listening Comprehension

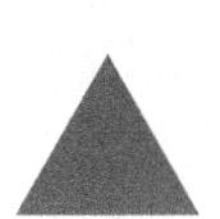   

Writing – Fiction

Think of a fiction story you would like to write. Draw a picture of the characters and setting of your fiction story. The tell or write a sentence telling about an event in the story.

High-Frequency Words

■	corn	come	ran
●	play	day	put
▲	arms	said	any

Phonics

 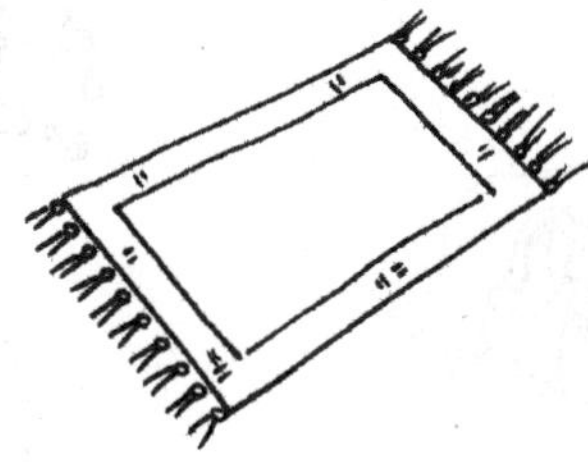  

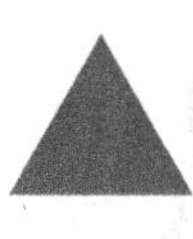   

Name______________________

Listening Comprehension

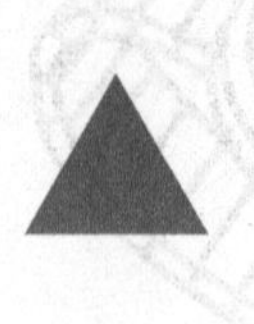   

Writing – Fiction

Think about a story from your life. Draw a picture that shows something that happened to you. Then make a list of three things that happened during that event.

High-Frequency Words

 moon   down   door

 her   his   where

 bad   here   how

Name

Phonics

High-Frequency Words

 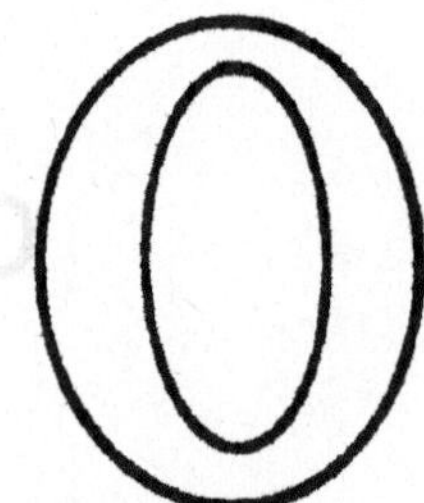  

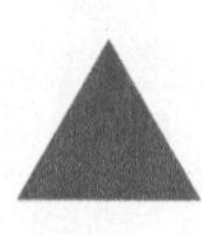   

38

Listening Comprehension

 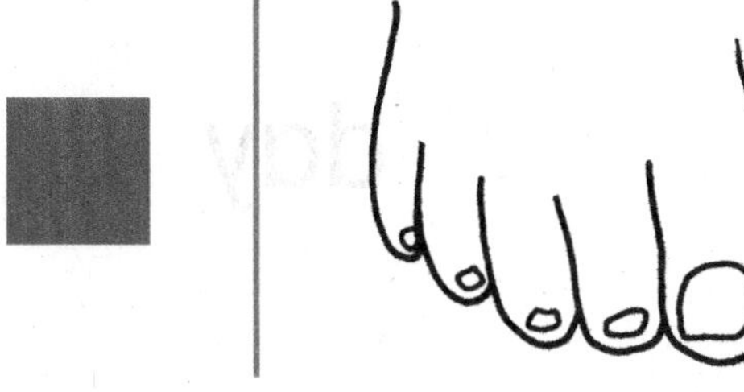  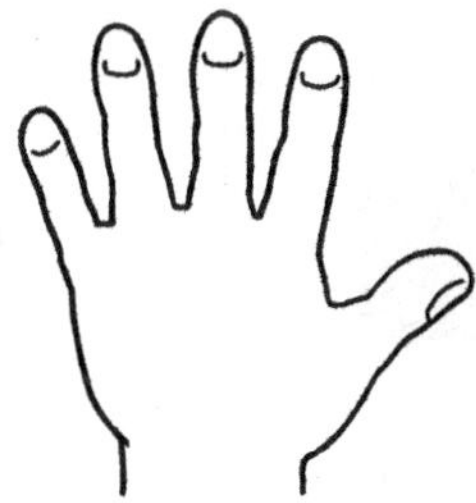

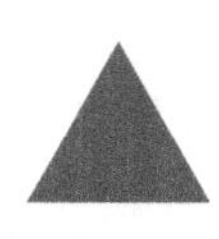   

 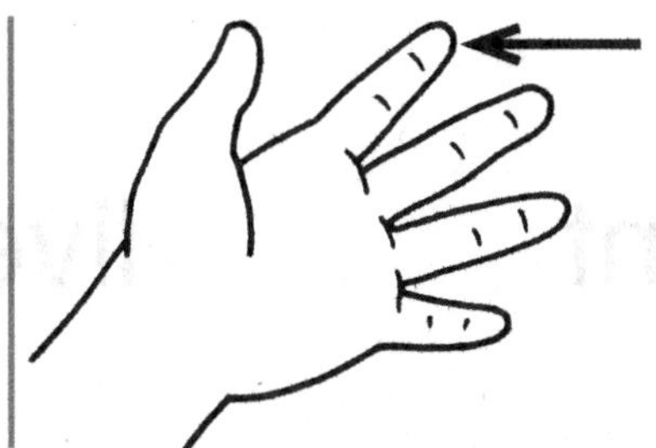 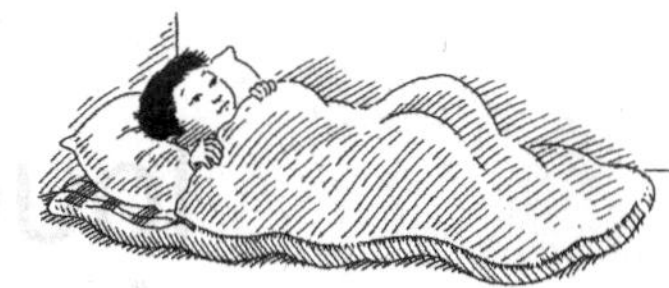

Writing – Fiction

Think about your favorite fiction book. Draw
a picture showing your favorite fiction book. Then
write or tell about the events at the beginning
and end of the book.

High-Frequency Words

　are　　away　　day

　give　　giant　　live

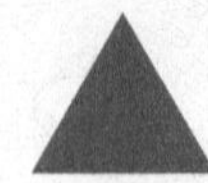　laugh　　middle　　little

Phonics

 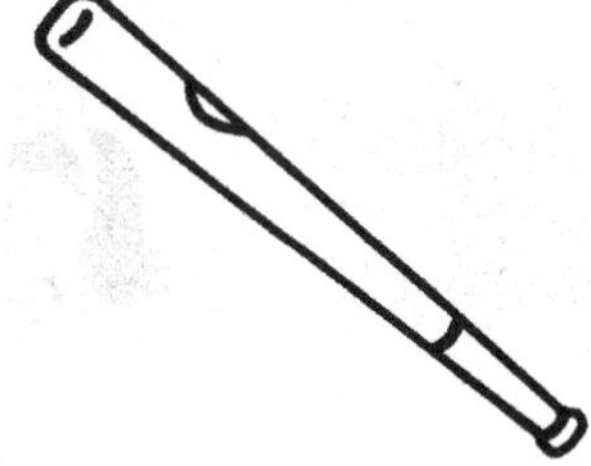 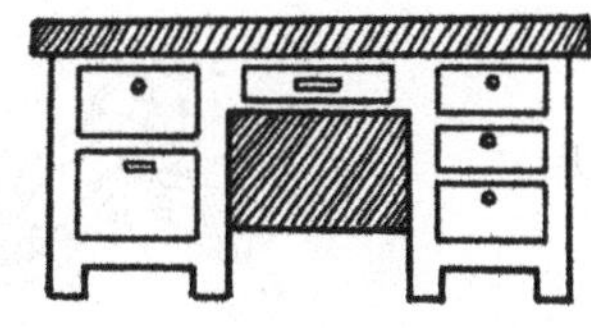 

  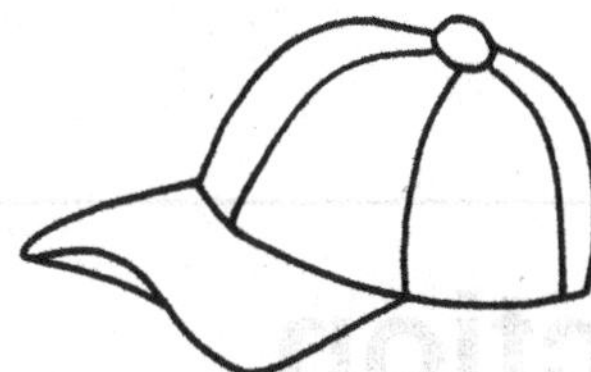 

Name_______________________

Listening Comprehension

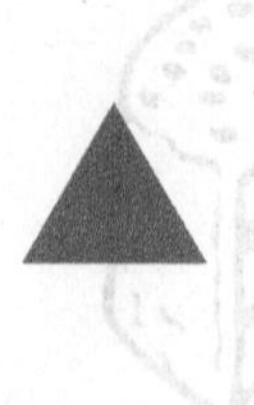   

Writing – Fiction

Draw a picture of a make-believe person you would like to tell a story about. Then write or tell one thing the person in your story would do.

42

High-Frequency Words

 sunny   funny   furry

 were   there   when

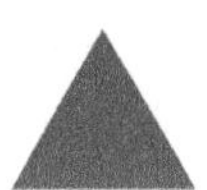 home   sun   some

Name _______________________

Phonics

 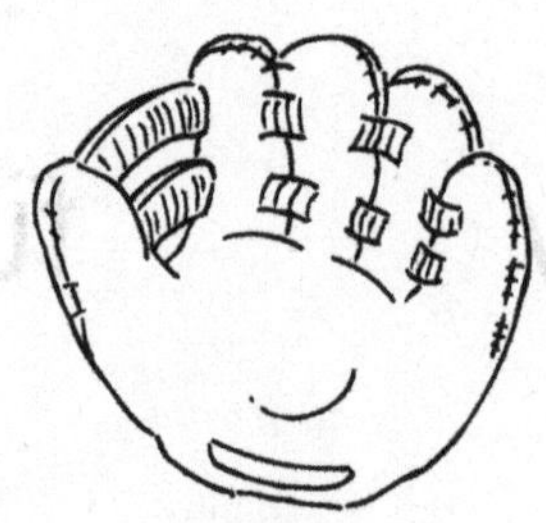 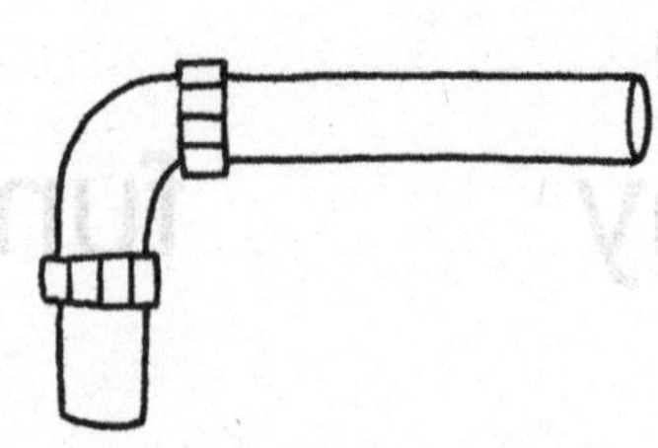 

   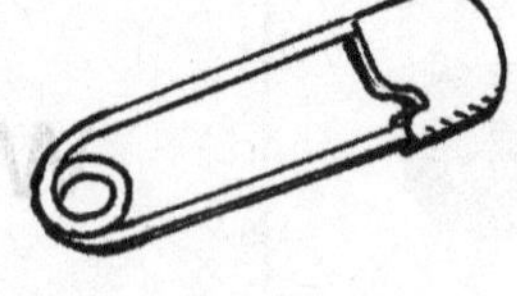

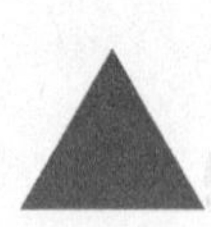   

 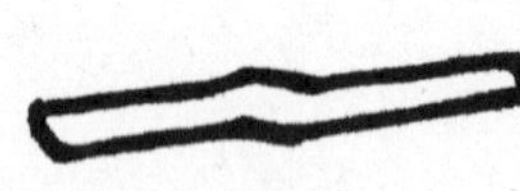 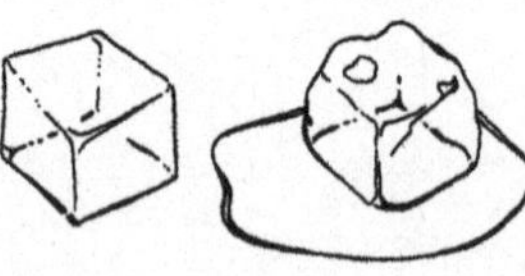 

Listening Comprehension

Writing – Fiction

Draw a picture of Pegasus, the flying horse from the story. Then write or tell something Pegasus could do in a story.

Name_______________

High-Frequency Words

 find   pin   far

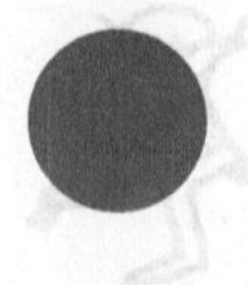 move   out   over

 age   when   again

Phonics

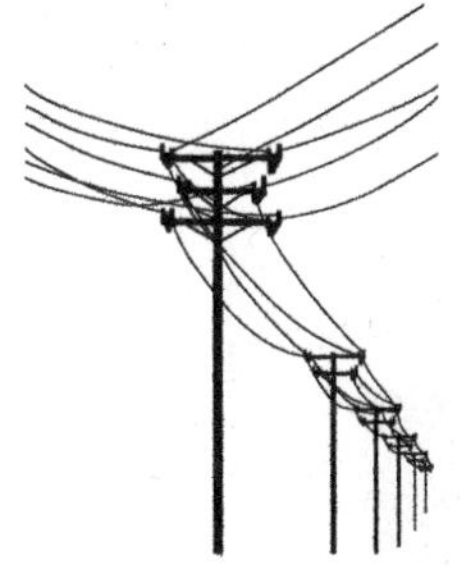

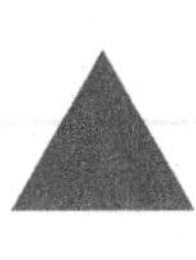   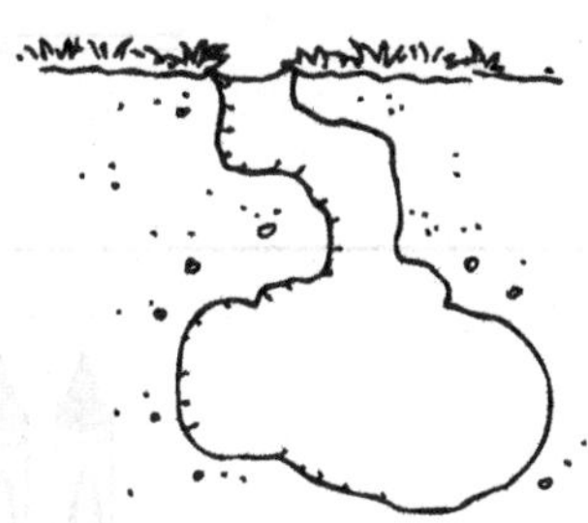

Name

Listening Comprehension

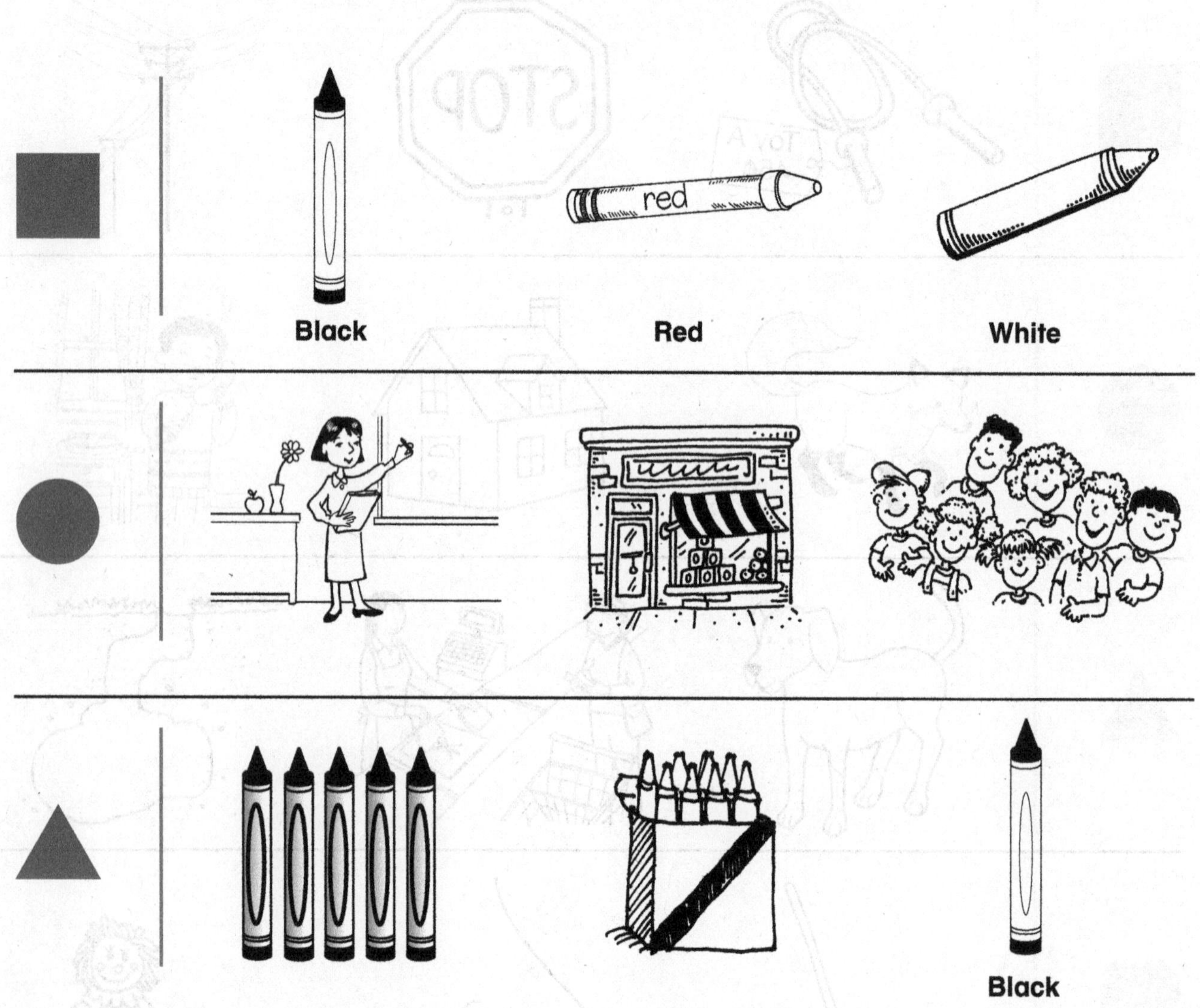

Writing – Narrative

On a separate sheet of paper, use crayons to draw what you most like to draw. Draw with your favorite color. Then write or tell about what you most like to draw and your favorite color.

High-Frequency Words

■	ball	all	any
●	cow	down	now
▲	pay	little	pretty

Name_______________

Phonics

 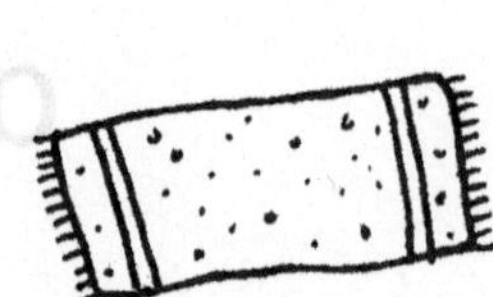 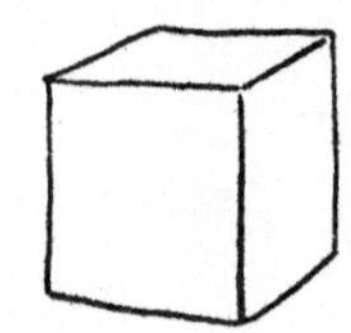 

  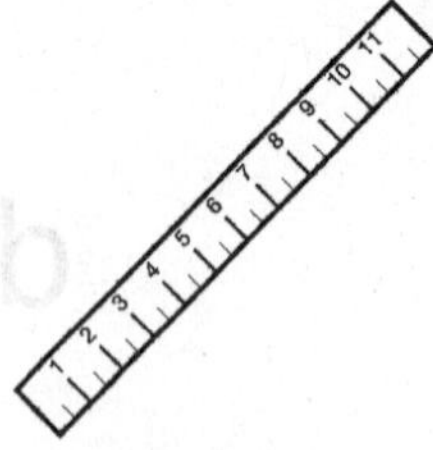 

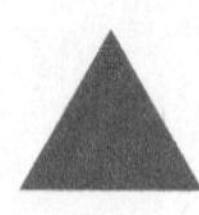   

Listening Comprehension

 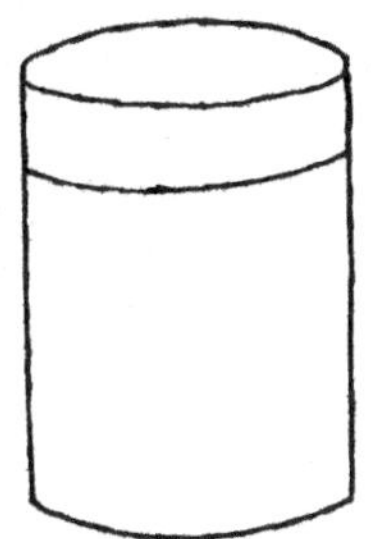  

   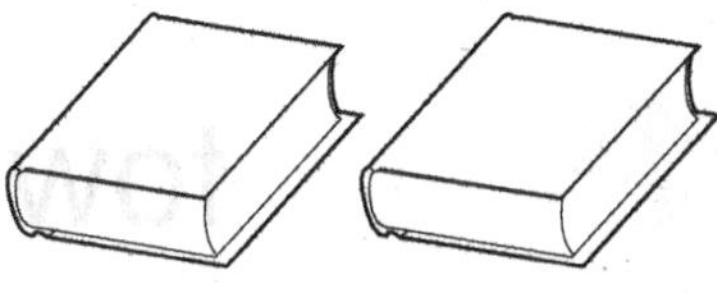

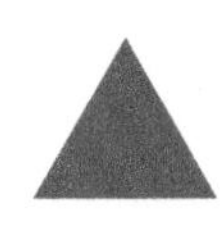   

Writing – Narrative

On a separate sheet of paper, draw a picture of your favorite place. Where is it? What does it look like? Write or tell about your favorite place.

High-Frequency Words

 sack   blue   black

 town   born   brown

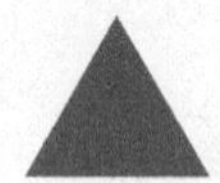 white   why   light

Phonics

 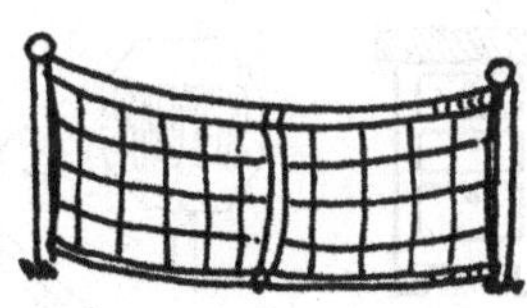  

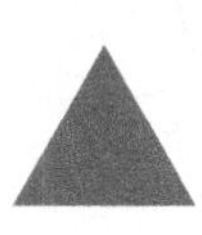   

   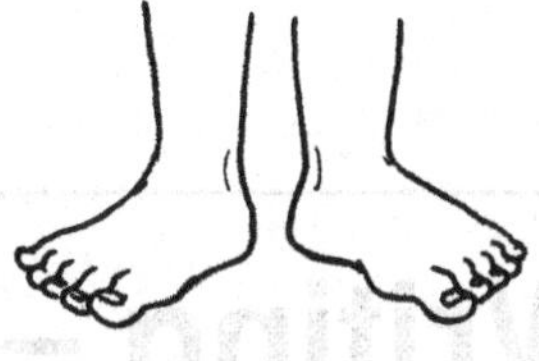

Name_______________________

Listening Comprehension

 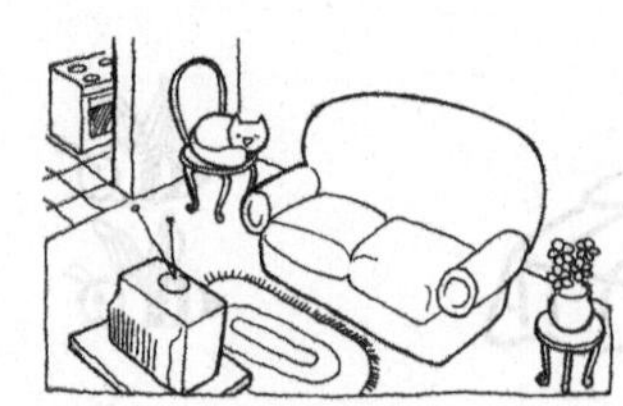  

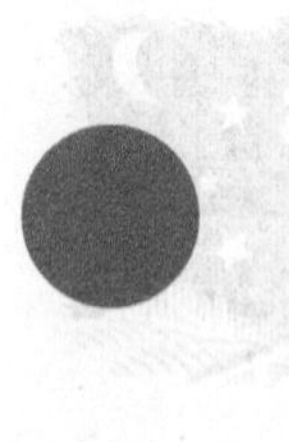  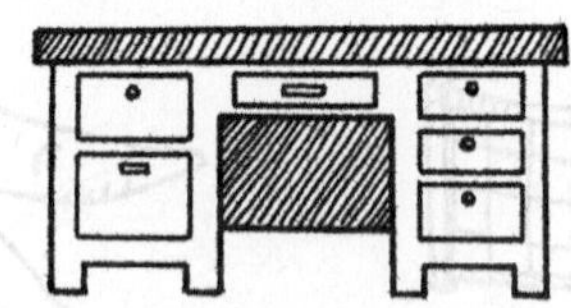 

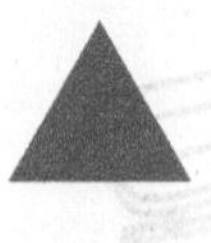 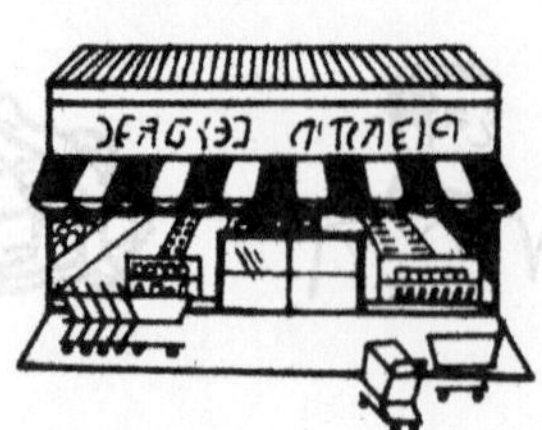  

Writing – Narrative

On a separate sheet of paper, draw a picture of a problem you had to solve. How did you solve the problem? Write or tell about the steps you took to solve the problem.

54

Name______________________________

High-Frequency Words

 food   good   got

 one   pin   open

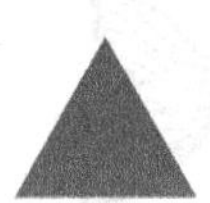 could   can   did

Name________________________

Phonics

 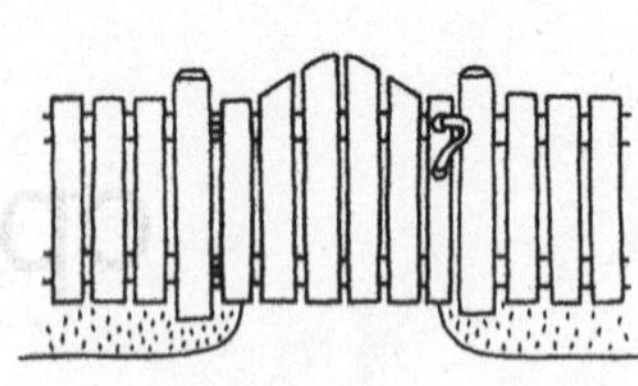  

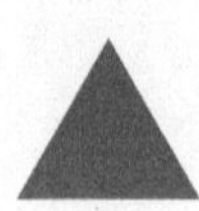 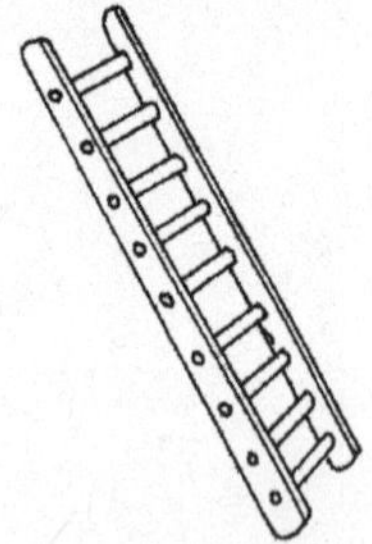  

Name_______________________________

Listening Comprehension

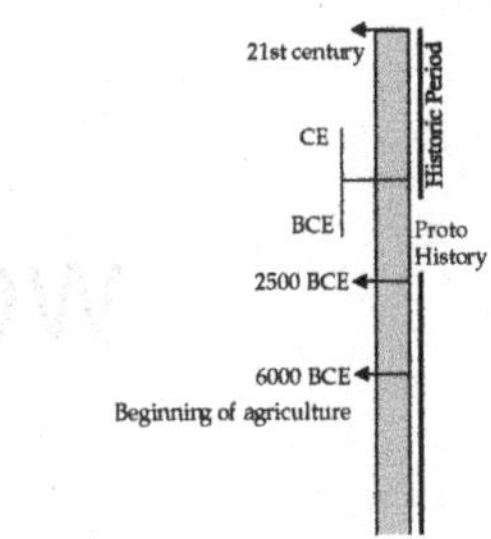

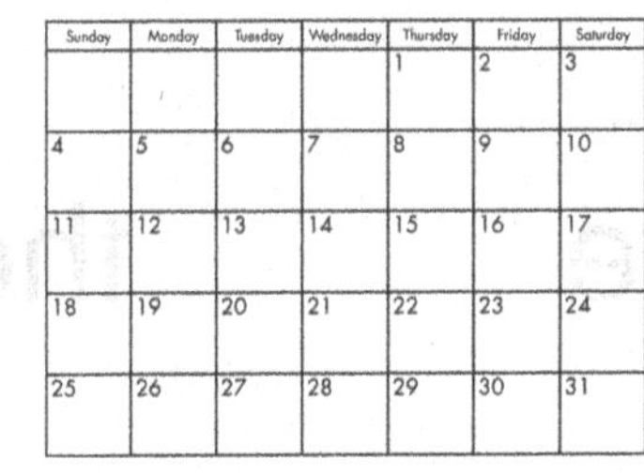

Writing – Narrative

On a separate sheet of paper, draw a picture about something you would like to do when you grow up. Then write or tell about what you would like to do when you grow up.

Name_______________

High-Frequency Words

 play   please   said

 wet   water   want

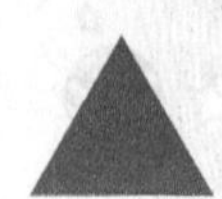 every   there   they

Phonics

   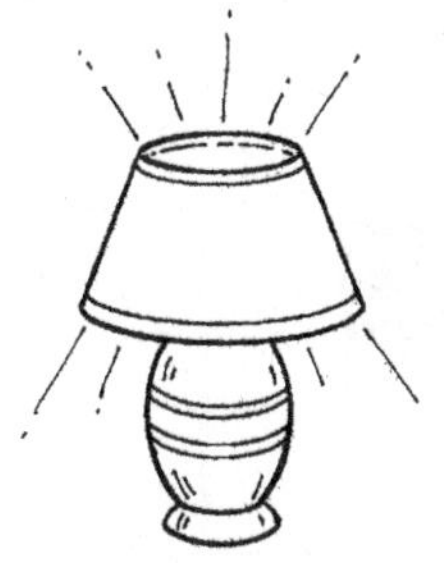

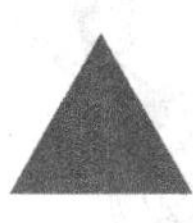   

  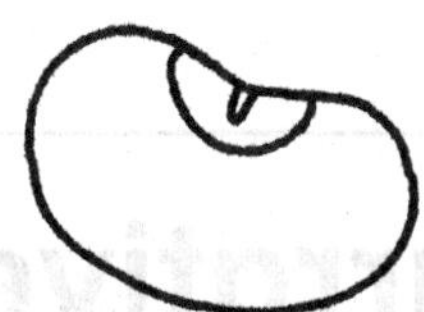 

Name________________

Listening Comprehension

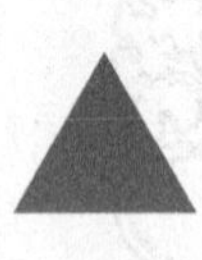   

Writing – Narrative

On a separate sheet of paper, draw a picture of a tradition that you have with your family. Write or tell two sentences about the tradition. Check to make sure the first letters of names have capital letters.

High-Frequency Words

■	boy	be	the
●	saw	want	she
▲	her	out	our

Phonics

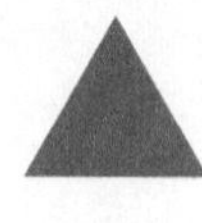

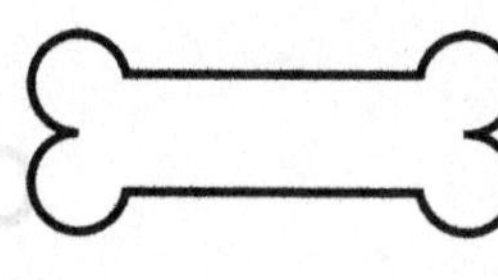

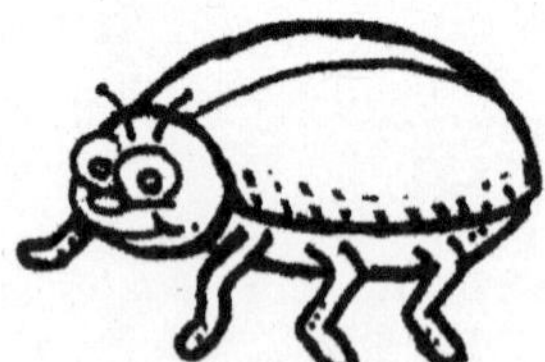

Listening Comprehension

 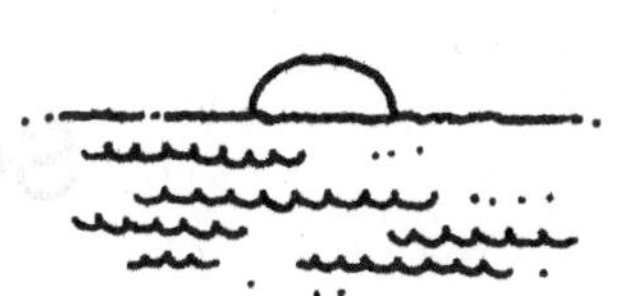  

   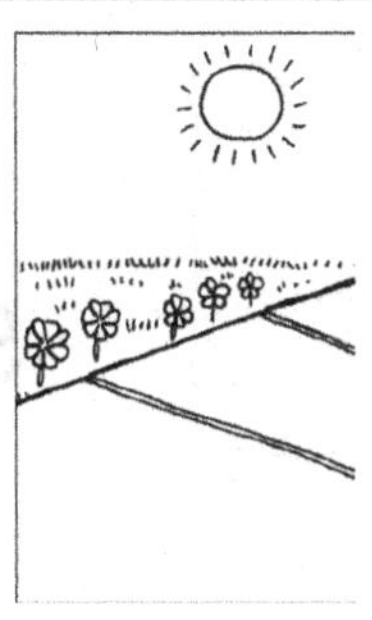

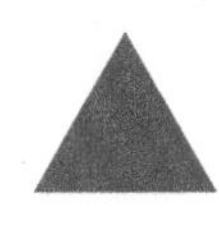   

Writing – Literary Nonfiction

You know that snow is a weather event. On
a separate sheet of paper, draw a picture
of a different weather event. Then write or
tell a question and an answer about that
weather event.

Name_______________

High-Frequency Words

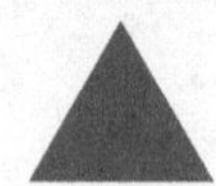

be   eat   see

soon   see   new

saw   week   walk

Phonics

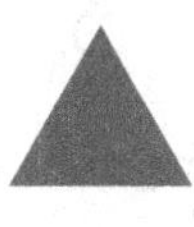   

Name_______________

Listening Comprehension

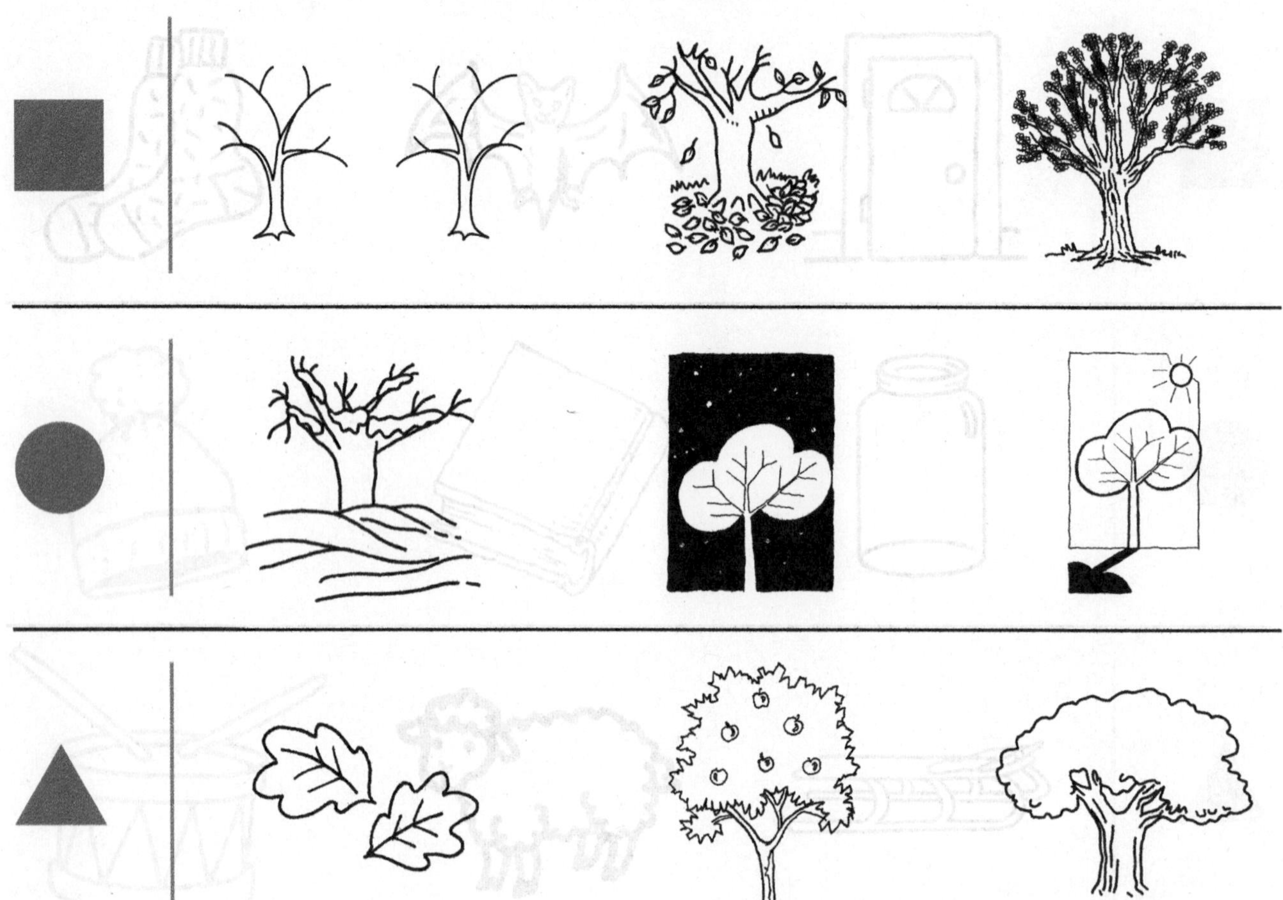

Writing – Literary Nonfiction

What might a tree look like during spring, summer, fall, or winter? On a separate sheet of paper, draw a picture of what a tree might look like during one of the seasons. Then write or tell a complete sentence about the tree.

High-Frequency Words

who   soon   why

into   do   one

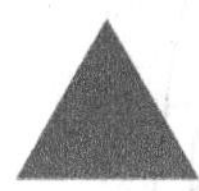

they   were   there

Phonics

   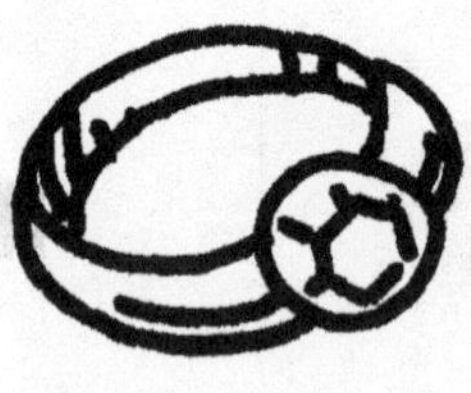

   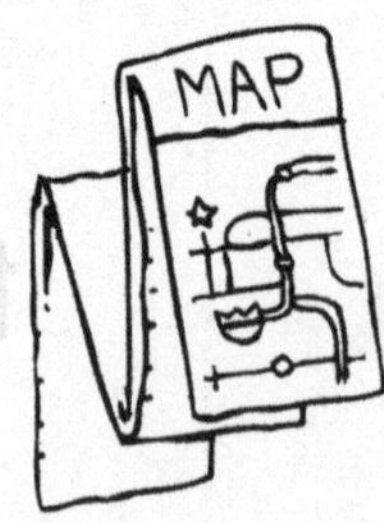

   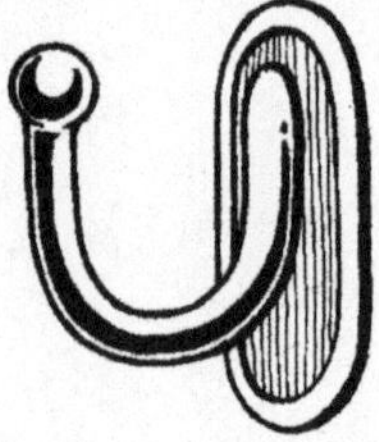

Listening Comprehension

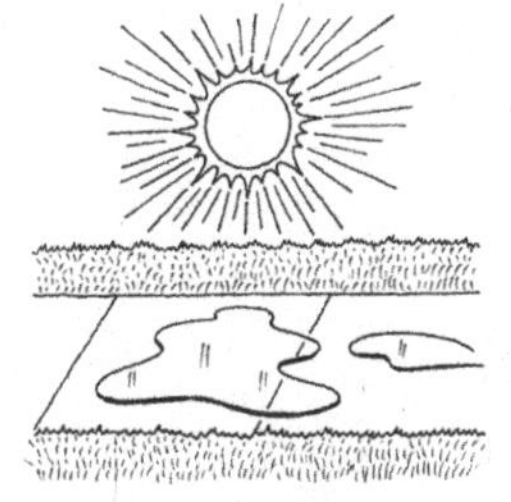  

Writing – Literary Nonfiction

On a separate sheet of paper, draw a picture of something you like to do when it rains. Then write or tell a complete sentence about what you like to do when it rains.

Name_______________________

High-Frequency Words

■	so	into	say
●	now	out	or
▲	can	that	then

Name _______________________________

Phonics

  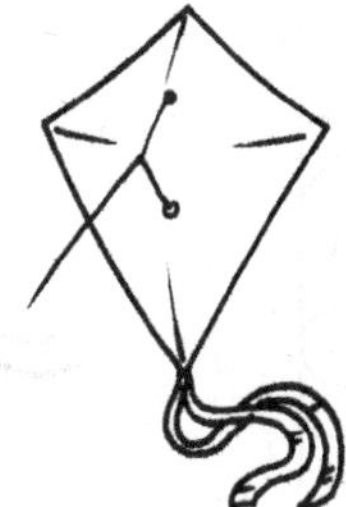 

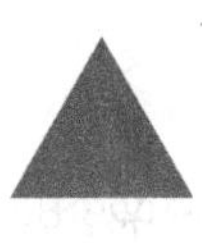   

Listening Comprehension

  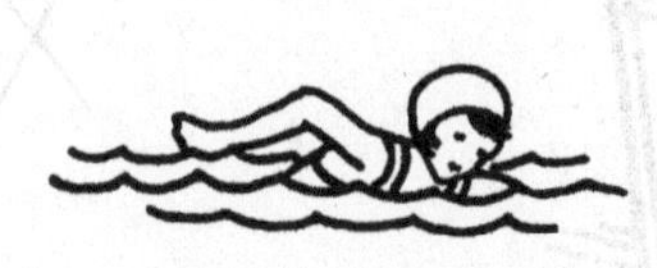 

 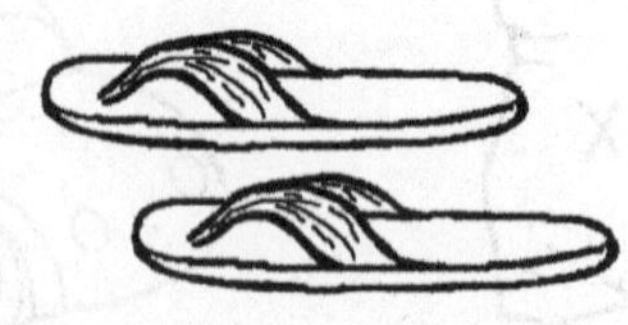  

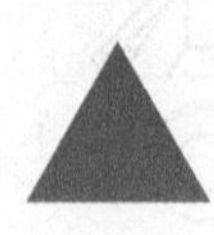   

Writing – Literary Nonfiction

On a separate sheet of paper, draw a picture of something you wear in the summer. Then write or tell a complete sentence about what you do when you are wearing it.

Unit 5 Week 4 Progress Check-Up

High-Frequency Words

■	new	not	blue
●	how	too	tell
▲	why	ten	when

Name______________________

Phonics

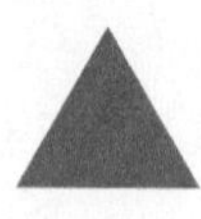   

  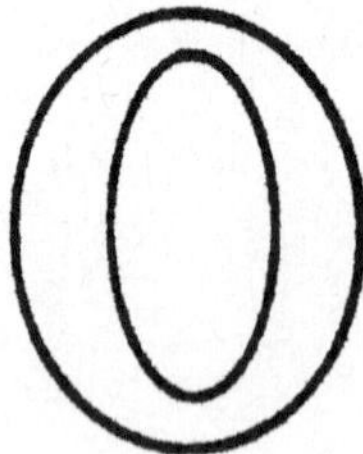 

74

Unit 5 Week 5 Progress Check-Up

Name _______________________________

Listening Comprehension

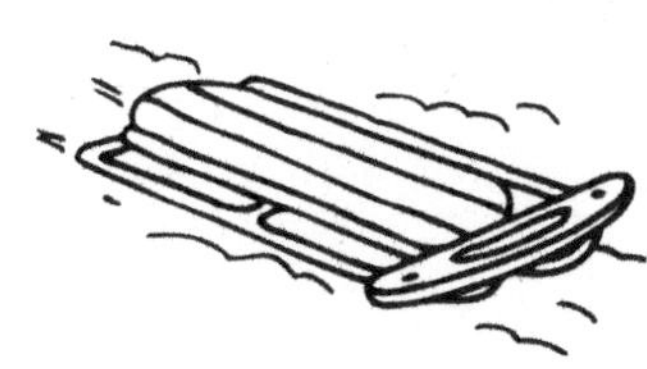

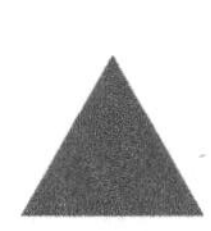

Writing – Literary Nonfiction

What might you do if it snowed? On a separate sheet of paper, draw a picture of what you might do if it snowed. Then write or tell a complete sentence telling what you might do if it snowed.

Unit 5 Week 5 Progress Check-Up